PROMISE AND PERILS

BASIC ISSUES IN CONTEMPORARY CIVILIZATION

by T. Walter Wallbank, Professor of History, University of Southern California

and Alastair M. Taylor, Professor of Political Studies and Geography, Queen's University

Library of Congress Card Number 66-14840
Copyright © 1966 by Scott, Foresman and Company. All Rights Reserved. Printed in the United States of America.

SCOTT, FORESMAN AND COMPANY

Chicago • *Atlanta* • *Dallas* • *Palo Alto* • *Fair Lawn, N. J.*

CONTENTS

901.94
WISP
80171
Oct 1972

INTRODUCTION

Freedom is not a reward or a decoration that is celebrated with champagne. . . . It's a chore, on the contrary, and a long-distance race, quite solitary and very exhausting. No champagne, no friends raising their glasses as they look at you affectionately. Alone in a forbidding room, alone in the prisoner's box before the judges, and alone to decide in the face of oneself or in the face of others' judgment. At the end of freedom is a court sentence.[1]

This description of "freedom" by the French novelist Albert Camus contrasts sharply with the uncomplicated and clarion declarations of liberty found in our traditional literature. True, our own century has been marked by affirmations of the "four freedoms"—and by demands throughout the Afro-Asian world to implement the principle of "one man, one vote." Yet in our complex age we have also learned, with Camus, that freedom cannot be a simple "reward" or goal in itself, but remains a "long-distance race" that can never end for mankind. Without freedom, life becomes intolerable—but its possession must in turn always expose us to the dilemmas of difficult choices—in short, to the promise and perils which together comprise the human condition.

It is our growing awareness of this dual nature of the basic problems of our times that sets the mood for much of contemporary civilization. It has been suggested that man has always found himself engaged simultaneously in three conflicts: with nature, with his fellow man, and with himself.[2] Science and technology have provided him with unprecedented freedom to initiate action in all three spheres. And the consequences of such action in today's world form the core of the pages that follow. Ultimately, the most revolutionary force in history is an idea—and rival ideologies war daily for the mastery of men's minds with their competing promises and price tags. The cry for freedom has raised banners across the Asian and African continents—and set aflame their villages. What will liberty ultimately bring them: law and economic advancement, or license and military adventures? Man's inhumanity to man has been a recurrent theme through the centuries: religious wars, racial persecution, pogroms, and the more subtle forms of discrimination and cruelty as blandly practiced by the status seekers of every age. Where does our sophisticated generation stand in these matters—what is its inventory of human rights, and societal wrongs?

And what are we earthlings doing with our environmental inheritance; how do we equate the exploitation of natural resources to satisfy immediate wants with their conservation for generations yet unborn? How many people can this planet support? How many should be supported? Just where do we strike the balance in this complex man-environment relationship? And what are the implications for us as individuals? Is the world now so complex and computerized that we no longer "count"? Are we little more than automata, or is each of us basically still autonomous?

From our Hellenic cultural legacy we derive the story of how Prometheus stole fire from the gods and gave mankind its gift with which to build civilization. For his audacity Prometheus was tortured—even as from our Hebraic legacy we learn of the consequences for man when he ate of the fruit of knowledge. These may be myths, but they provide insight into the human condition, namely, that *Homo sapiens* is endowed with *logos,* or the reasoning faculty, with which he must ever seek answers to both the "how" and "why" of his relationship to the cosmos, to his fellow man, and to his inner nature. The application of reason has built-in promise and perils—as Prometheus and Adam alike discovered. In today's world, as their descendants, we, too, have to live with the agony and the glory. If the older, Eden-like concept of "paradise" is gone forever, it is because *Homo sapiens* has the Promethean knowledge to immolate the planet in a thermonuclear fireball. But it can also assist him to build the New Jerusalem.

1

The War for Men's Minds:

THE CHANGING FACTS
OF INTERNATIONAL LIFE

The World in 1945

In the closing period of World War II, few observers other than Winston Churchill anticipated the onset of a gigantic confrontation of rival ideologies in international affairs and the emerging bitter struggle for men's minds. As the global conflict ended in 1945, the expectation existed of cooperation among the victors. Above all, there was to be a new era of amity between the Soviet Union and the United States. Despite the discouraging setbacks that parliamentary democracy suffered between 1919 and 1945, there was renewed promise of its vigor and advance in the world. Fascism had been overwhelmed; its victims in Europe now could regain their freedom; and the Nationalist Chinese, so long under Japanese attack, could renew the task of building their nation and of widening its democratic institutions. Many believed that self-determination for the millions of people living under colonial rule would ensure political stability, Western parliamentary rule, and economic progress. The capstone of this new structure in world affairs was to be the United Nations. It was fervently hoped that this new international organization (better planned than its predecessor, the League of Nations) would constitute insurance against future wars and that it would also serve as a center where all nations would harmoniously work together to improve the lot of mankind.

The hopes of many were quickly dashed, however, when the Cold War began in 1946. This conflict, neither outright war nor actual peace, was to a large extent an outgrowth of Joseph Stalin's suspicions of the West and his desire to subvert and conquer the non-Communist World. The countries of Eastern Europe emerged from Nazi rule only to become Soviet satellites. In Asia, Nationalist China witnessed the defeat of Japan but collapsed in 1949 before the Communist offensive of Mao Tse-tung, the father of Chinese Communism. While Stalin lived, the U.S.S.R. was the unchallenged leader of the world Communist movement and the ultimate arbiter of Marxist ideology. Communist China, while never a subservient satellite, long accepted Soviet aid, its essential primacy, and some of its advice. The United Nations became a casualty of this Cold War. Constructive programs were often blocked in the Security Council by the Soviet veto, and angry exchanges disturbed any spirit of harmony.

Meanwhile, the nations of Western Europe emerged in 1945 impoverished and psychologically drained. There was much war devastation in France, and incredibly more in Germany. In fact, all of Western Europe, victor and vanquished alike, needed massive economic aid and, if further Russian encroachments were to be avoided, substantial military support from the United States. Both needs were generously supplied as America assumed the role of unchallenged leader and economic benefactor in Western Europe. The world was now dominated by two power systems, that of the Free World led by the United States, and that of the Communist Bloc under the aegis of the Soviet Union. This bipolar situation was to last until the late 1950's.

Fragmentation of the Communist Bloc

In less than two decades the world picture has changed radically. One of the most significant developments has been the growing disunity in the Russian-dominated Communist system brought about mainly by the open break between China and the U.S.S.R. In essence, this rupture has mirrored a Sino-Soviet struggle for leadership of the international Communist movement. On the surface it has been doctrinal, but the ideological polemics have concealed the clash of basic national interests. The quarrel may have begun as early as 1956 when Nikita Khrushchev, then the First Secretary of the Communist party, gave his famous speech denouncing Stalin and his excesses. After securing the premiership in 1958, Khrushchev accelerated his program of de-Stalinization, defended the peaceful and evolutionary path to Communism, and supported the policy of coexistence with the non-Communist World. Chinese leaders were affronted by this repudiation of Stalinism, and the gulf between Peking and Moscow progressively widened. While Chinese Communist ideology became more radical, as evidenced by its adoption of the commune system, the Soviet Union appeared to move in the opposite direction. It disapproved of the communes and denied the Chinese contention that they should be the model for the whole Communist World.

Determined to force Peking's adherence to Soviet policy, Khrushchev withdrew all 3000 of his technicians from China and cut off other Soviet aid. In 1960 at an international conclave of some 81 Communist parties, China and Russia exchanged bitter denunciations. Then in 1962 the U.S.S.R. failed to support Communist China's attack on India. As a result of the border war with India that ensued for a short time, China occupies 14,500 square miles of Indian territory in the Himalayan Mountains. Furthermore, after the American and Soviet confrontation over Cuba (in which the Soviet Union backed down) Peking bitterly accused Khrushchev of "adventurism" and "capitulationism." From 1962 the quarrel mounted in intensity. A barrage of public denunciations against the Russian brand of Communism was fired by China and elicited equally vituperative responses. After Khrushchev's fall from power in late 1964 his successors, Leonid Brezhnev and Alexei Kosygin, attempted to heal the growing breach between the U.S.S.R. and Communist China. But neither conferences with Communist China's Premier Chou En-lai in the Soviet Union nor Brezhnev's subsequent visit to Communist China, North Vietnam, and Korea resolved the differences. Evidence of the depth of the Sino-Soviet rift came with the March 1965 meeting in Moscow of 19 pro-Soviet Communist parties. The conclave was called by the U.S.S.R. in an effort to reassert its position as the leader of world Communism, but Communist China and its supporters refused to attend. Even the aerial attacks by the United States and South Vietnam upon North Vietnam have not yet pushed the two Communist giants back together. The U.S.S.R., to the consternation of Communist China, has hesitated to take a strong stand against the United States with which it has sought better relations. Peking's militant position on southeast Asia has been calculated to arouse the hostility of peoples toward the West, especially the United States, and to test the decision-makers in Moscow who have to weigh the advantages of a further *détente* on the one hand and a chance of losing leadership in Communism's campaign to maneuver the Afro-Asians into an anti-Western stance.

One of the basic factors underlying this feud is the difference in the stage of Communist development in the two countries. The Soviet Union has surmounted the initial painful period of industrialization and has achieved the status of a great world power. The original urge for world revolution has subsided somewhat as its masses have become eager for higher standards of living. Soviet Russia has much to lose from any major conflict—the destruction of an immense industrial complex created by great effort and sacrifice. China, in the early and revolutionary stage of Communist transformation, decries Russian timidity. Peking is ready to support enthusiastically "national liberation struggles" in Asia, Latin America, and Africa. Its leaders believe that limited revolutionary wars can be fought without much danger of escalation and that China would survive even a nuclear world war with the United States. Mao Tse-tung and his colleagues criticize the U.S.S.R. for aiding non-Communist states such as India and for sending substantial amounts of economic aid to Afro-Asian nations rather than to China. Premier Khrushchev was bitterly accused of being so eager for a *détente* with the United States that he callously neglected Chinese interests. In short, Khrushchev's de-Stalinization program and his policy of peaceful coexistence in China's opinion constituted infidelity to true Marxism. And his successors have not been thought of any more highly.

Aside from this doctrinal breach, there is an important historical background of clashing national interests. The Chinese resent Russian annexation of large slices of their territory in the eighteenth and nineteenth centuries. Peking has irredentist claims to areas now under Soviet control or influence, such as Outer Mongolia and the maritime area with its important port of Vladivostock. Armed clashes have been reported taking place on the long Sino-Soviet border, to which both nations have moved large numbers of troops. And Chinese hackles rise over memories of Stalin's arbitrary interference in the affairs of the Chinese Communist party. As for Soviet Russia, it undoubtedly feels some apprehension over the designs of an expansionist and truculent neighbor, burdened with supporting a population of more than 700,000,000. To add to growing Soviet trepidation, Communist China conducted its first atomic test in 1964 and a second the following year.

A product, in part of the Sino-Soviet feud and in part of changing times, has been the erosion of Russian controls in the east European satellites. Russia imposed her authority on Czechoslovakia, Poland, Hungary, Rumania, Bulgaria, Albania, and Yugoslavia after World War II. Under Stalinist rule a kind of "collectivistic nightmare" followed. Yugoslavia, however, was able to break away from the Moscow orbit in 1948 and to follow its own brand of national Communism. Following Khrushchev's rise to power in 1953, a more lenient Russian policy was initiated toward the satellites, and a number of Stalinist leaders were demoted. But a little freedom proved to be a dangerous thing.

In 1956 a serious revolt in Hungary was suppressed by Russian troops and tanks, and riots occurred in Poland. The emergence of the Sino-Soviet quarrel, however, has given the satellites a measure of bargaining power vis-à-vis the U.S.S.R. which now has to court the support of their respective Communist parties. Albania broke away completely from Moscow's control and accepted the protection of Peking. In 1958 Soviet troops were withdrawn from Rumania, which has subsequently gained a substantial measure of freedom. Trade relations have been cultivated with the West, and Soviet efforts to subordinate Rumania's economy to the direction of a central planning body (Comecon) have been successfully resisted. Rumania has tried to mediate the dispute between the Soviet Union and Communist China. The de-Stalinization in Poland which followed the riots of 1956 has been partially reversed. Yet, under Poland's atheistic regime, Catholicism flourishes and agricultural collectivization has been repudiated. In practically all the so-called satellites similar signs of the corrosion of Russian authority and traditional Communist ideology are strikingly apparent.

A new fluidity in relations with the U.S.S.R. has thus developed in Eastern Europe, but at present there is no possibility of a complete break with Moscow. The satellite regimes are bound to the Soviet Union by economic and fraternal ties and by a military alliance, the Warsaw Pact. The East German government, for example, is dependent for its continuance upon Soviet support. Poland fears West German irredentism, while Czechoslovakia relies heavily upon Russian markets for her manufactured goods. By tradition there is a strong Slavic bond between Bulgaria and the Soviet Union, and Hungary looks to the U.S.S.R. for support in safeguarding the interests of the large Hungarian minority under Rumanian rule.

Tensions Within the Atlantic Alliance

Just as the unity of the Communist Bloc has been undermined, a somewhat comparable situation has developed in the Free World. The preservation of freedom and the recovery of economic health were made possible largely because of the military power and the Marshall Plan of the United States. In 1949 the military alliance for the defense of Western Europe, the North Atlantic Treaty Organization (NATO), was established under Washington's leadership. Europeans, conscious of their military impotence and economic weakness, were happy to recognize the dominant role of the United States in west European affairs. But this imbalance of power has changed in little more than a decade. By the early 1960's, Western Europe in general had made a significant recovery. The economic progress registered by the six members of the European Economic Community (Common Market) generally has been substantial. Exports have risen to new heights, gold reserves have mounted, and a buoyant spirit of confidence and self-assertion has marked the emergence of a revitalized Western Europe. Quarrels within the Communist Bloc have also reduced fear of any menace from Eastern Europe.

These developments have led, however, to new and disturbing problems within the Atlantic Alliance, the defense bastion of the Free World. In particular, questions have arisen as to what the role of the United States should be in Europe and how far the process of integration, initiated by the Common Market, should go. The basic aims of the initial European Economic Community were thought to be reconciliation between

France and Germany, the creation of a Common Market to help raise living standards, and the restoration of European prestige and influence in the world. It has been widely believed that the last objective can only be realized by the achievement of some form of European political union.

The United States since 1960 has attempted to work out a new relationship with Europe (especially in the realm of defense) that would satisfy the European desire for more equality with their American partner. Thus the United States has encouraged the goal of political unity. In the defense field, it advanced the idea of the Multilateral Force (MLF). This plan was designed to make possible the sharing of American atomic missiles with NATO members and thus largely to satisfy West Germany's desire to achieve some sort of nuclear involvement without permitting it to obtain nuclear initiative. Originally a force of twenty-five Polaris submarines was to be created and manned by international crews but with the United States retaining ultimate control over the atomic triggers. This force was later changed to surface vessels.

Such objectives have been seriously hindered by the policies of President Charles de Gaulle. This towering figure, presiding over the destiny of a renascent France that has been experiencing a rising birth rate, a dynamic economy, and a spirited air of national confidence, has been determined to reestablish the glory—and *"grandeur"*—of his nation. He has wished to secure its leadership in Europe and to decrease if not eliminate the influence of the "Anglo-Saxons," i.e., Great Britain and the United States, in Continental affairs. It was De Gaulle who in 1963 vetoed Britain's entry into the European Common Market, a decision in effect not to share any leadership with Great Britain on the Continent. Despite assurances that the United States would protect its Western allies with atomic missiles, Charles de Gaulle has reservations about America's commitment and has maintained that Continental Europe also needs to have its own atomic weapons. In justifying his position, De Gaulle has pointed to the late entry of the United States into both world wars and our recognition of the Vichy government. France is willing to provide Europe with a nuclear striking force. While still small, this atomic capability has helped to further French leadership and prestige on the Continent.

President de Gaulle is anxious to have the backing of an organized Europe but without ceding any freedom of action on the part of France. His idea of a European Union is a Europe of sovereign nations with some coordinating machinery. He sees the Community of the Six as an organization which, led by France, will enhance Europe's power, but he does not visualize it as the means to close political unity. With consummate skill De Gaulle has blocked and seemingly killed the American plan of MLF (to the relief of Great Britain and Canada which have strong reservations about it) and has advanced the posture and spirit of France in world affairs. General de Gaulle has refused to sign the Atomic Test Ban Treaty agreed to by the United States, the Soviet Union, and many other nations. He opposes American military efforts in South Vietnam on the grounds that he does not believe the United States can win a war there and that the solution for all of southeast Asia is neutralization. He has recognized Communist China and declared his determination not to become involved in any large war in Asia. He is trying, furthermore, to improve France's relations with the Soviet Union. Events of the next decade in Western Europe should be decisive. Will De Gaulle successfully obstruct efforts to effectively unite Europe and what, if any, role will Britain play in Continental affairs? Additionally can some mutually helpful and satisfactory relationship between the United States and its NATO allies be achieved, one that recognizes the new power and aspirations of Europe?

The Struggle for Men's Minds

While difficult questions remain to be answered in the Free World, the divisive trends in Communist ranks seem to be much deeper and more far reaching. A number of politically democratic systems are functioning in most of Western Europe, the United States, Canada, and Australia. It should be noted that even in these areas, in the economic field, traditional concepts of laissez faire are fast retreating before those of the welfare state.

The present antithesis of the more democratic nations is Communist China. Completely totalitarian in its use of power, and wholly collectivistic in its economy, Peking may exceed the worst actions of the U.S.S.R. under Stalin. Between these two extremes—one the Free World and the other Communist China—are the east European satellites of Soviet Russia that have veered away from Leninist-Stalinist ideology. The young generation in these satellite nations, because of increased contacts with the outside world, has doubts about Communist ideology. This is not to imply that democracy, Western style, is a possibility in the near future; but change is in the air. Reforms in the direction of further liberalization seem likely in most of the Soviet east European satellites.

The Soviet Union cannot be placed in the same ideological category as Communist China. During the Khrushchev era there was a carefully controlled lessening of the severities of Stalin's regime. No discernible shift away from this policy can be seen under Brezhnev and Kosygin, and it seems unlikely that there will be a reversion to the pre-Khrushchev severities. One of the basic flaws, however, in Soviet authoritarianism remains: the absence of any machinery for the constitutional transfer of power.

Similar in some ways to both the democratic and the authoritarian systems, the newly independent Afro-Asian regimes generally have preferred non-alignment in foreign affairs where such a choice has been possible. While most are one-party states, they cannot be compared with

Communist-totalitarian nations, for some of the spirit and the trappings of traditional Western democracy remain. The political instability and economic frustration in the underdeveloped world present a wide-open field for rivalry between Western democracy and the three current forms of Communism: Russian, Chinese, and eastern European satellite.

The strongest ideological and revolutionary thrust into the Afro-Asian world is now that of Communist China. For the first time in its history, China is a real factor in world-wide affairs, from Cuba to the Congo and eastward to South Vietnam. It is *the* major Asian power; it now has the atomic bomb, and hegemony in eastern Asia is perhaps within its grasp. In the ex-colonial areas Chinese influence is greater than that of Moscow because mainland China can employ the racial issue and thus take the role of the foremost spokesman against "white imperialism." By using its 10,000,000 Muslim Chinese to stress its sympathy with Islam, Communist China is increasing its contacts and influence with the nations of the Middle East.

Perhaps most striking has been China's entry into the confused and chaotic situation in Africa. Loans and technical assistance agreements have been made, African leaders have visited Peking, and Premier Chou En-lai has visited Africa. In fact, Communist China has more embassies in Africa than in all the rest of the world. Rebel forces in the Congo are receiving Peking's support in their faltering struggle against the government in Leopoldville. The continent of Africa may become the arena for a violent clash in ideology, not so much between the West and the Soviet Union, as between the latter and mainland China.

The most critical struggle and immediate challenge of Chinese Communism has been in southeast Asia. Using North Vietnam as its agent, Peking has threatened to bring much of this area within its orbit of control. It is significant that Chinese maps show Burma, Vietnam, Korea, and Thailand, as well as Nepal, Bhutan, Sikkim, and part of the Soviet Maritime Far Eastern Provinces as Chinese territory.

The Multipower World of the 1960's

In international affairs the mid-1960's has witnessed the end of a bipolar world and the return to a multipower international system. The former clear-cut ideological confrontation between East and West has become cloudy and muddled. This situation was illustrated when the Soviet Union provided India, a parliamentary and non-aligned nation, with arms against China and when Pakistan, a stoutly Muslim religious state, veered toward Marxist China because of the quarrel with New Delhi over Kashmir. When Soviet Russia accused China of having "imperialistic ambitions" and of "inflaming nationalistic passions in central Asia," this was not the voice of the leader of world Communism but that of a national state primarily interested in protecting its vital interests.

The Cold War of the late 1940's and 1950's has taken on new facets which involve dangers and opportunities for the West. The battle between Communism and democracy continues with the final issue in doubt. The international facts of life add up in the 1960's to a complex and dangerous, but far from hopeless, situation for the West. Unlike the early phases of the Cold War, the U.S.S.R. faces not only a potent America but also a confident and powerful Europe. In addition, her satellites are no longer submissive agents of Soviet policy. And her former powerful ally, China, is now an ominous rival. The fanaticism and revolutionary expansionism of Communist China is profoundly disturbing. Yet it may open up new possibilities of cooperation between not only the Free World and the heretofore non-aligned states but even with members of the non-Chinese Communist Bloc. In all of this new fluidity in world affairs lie opportunities for United States foreign policy, utilizing infinite patience and delicacy backed by strength. One disturbing factor, however, has been the intensification of the ideological and military struggle in South Vietnam, for the commitment of large forces by Washington to assist the South Vietnamese government may yet draw the two rival Communist leaders closer together.

Topics for Discussion:

1. Discuss whether the decline of Russian control over the satellites implies that the ideology of nationalism in Eastern Europe is proving stronger than that of communism?
2. Analyze the relative importance of the following factors in explaining Communist China's challenge to Soviet Russia: (1) Marxian ideology, (2) the assertion of national status, and (3) China's objectives in international power politics.
3. What actions has Moscow taken to counter Peking's challenge to its leadership of the international Communist movement?
4. Do you think Great Britain will eventually become politically and economically tied to Continental Europe? What are the arguments for and against such ties?
5. What do you envisage as the future association of the United States with Europe? How can De Gaulle's suspicion of the "Anglo-Saxons" be explained? If you were French, how would you feel toward Great Britain and the United States?
6. Do you believe De Gaulle is justified in his contention that France can and should lead Europe? Must Europe have one nation lead it, and if so, is there any country in Europe other than France that could take this role?
7. How can the United States increase fruitful points of contact with the east European satellites?

8. Should the United States continue to remain hostile to Communist China while endeavoring to be more conciliatory to Soviet Russia or should the policy be the exact reverse? Discuss what can be gained by either policy and what other course might be pursued.

9. Now that Communist China has the atomic bomb, should the United States support its entrance into the UN and establish closer diplomatic contacts in order to secure Peking's membership in the Test Ban Treaty? What would Communist China have to gain by signing the treaty? Are there any similarities between the positions of France and China on this issue?

10. Should the U.S. continue to send foreign aid to countries such as Egypt, whose leaders revile it and whose people sack and burn its facilities? Using this as a starting point, discuss the pros and cons of America giving foreign aid. What has America achieved by giving foreign aid and what can it hope to gain in the future?

11. In trying to police the world has the United States attempted to do too much and achieved no more than what Walter Lippmann calls "scatteration"? How much policing can and should the U.S. do?

12. What reasonable alternatives exist for the United States in South Vietnam, where victory seems unattainable without the commitment of nearly 500,000 American troops and evacuation is unacceptable?

2

Nationalism and
Expanding Loyalties

Nationalism's Historic Role

Nationalism has been one of the most dynamic factors in the development of the modern world. It can be defined as the loyalty and devotion of an individual to a group with common ties of language, race, culture, religion, or historical tradition; in modern times this group has usually been a state. Nationalism generally involves pride in belonging to a particular political unit and a feeling of superiority over other groups. This last characteristic has occasionally been allied to racialism, a form of "biological nationalism."

Modern nationalism is primarily the development of Western peoples. Since the late Middle Ages it has been an instrument of progress. Nationalism was a positive force in the creation of nations out of the numerous petty and antagonistic feudal states. In this way it helped to increase the efficiency of government and the development of larger units of human cooperation. Nationalism has also enriched world civilization, not only in the area of its genesis, but in all parts of the world where its ideology has taken root. It has been a vehicle for plenteousness and variety in the many patterns of national culture, and has given meaning and distinctiveness to the lives of the members of national groups.

On occasion nationalism has provided the essential defensive spirit that enables people to withstand aggression, as in the case of Churchill's Great Britain; or clandestinely, as in France during World War II when the resistance movement continued to oppose Nazi tyranny.

But twentieth-century historical forces and their resultant problems have created a world in which the traditional role of nationalism is being reviewed. There is ample evidence attesting to the need for newer and wider forms of political, cultural, and economic cooperation between all peoples than is possible within the sovereign-state systems. There is, for example, an urgent need for the widest common effort to reduce the economic imbalance between the rich industrialized nations, on the one hand, and the poor underdeveloped states, on the other, by raising the economic level of the latter.

International partnership is a rapidly growing need in both science and medicine. Within these fields there is a logical advantage to having international cooperation in the peaceful use of atomic energy, in space exploration and communication, and in the conservation and utilization of the earth's natural resources. All peoples have an interest in a common effort to curb the world's ominous population explosion. And in the political field the potential destructiveness of nuclear weapons demands more effective international control.

In spite of the urgency for cooperation on the widest scale on these and other common problems of mankind, the contemporary world unfortunately presents many examples of narrow loyalties, reactionary national rivalries and suspicions, and the inability, on the part of what the English historian Arnold Toynbee has dubbed the "national fractions of the human race," to shelve divisive and largely outworn national stereotypes in favor of many vitally needed international undertakings.

Ireland and Palestine Partitioned

Ireland is a good case in point. This small island, endowed so meagerly with natural resources, has a total population of little more than four million. It forms a natural strategic, economic, and cooperative unit with its larger neighboring island, Great Britain. Yet the events of the past have sundered this natural unity. Ireland is partitioned. In the north are the six Ulster counties, the majority of whose population are the descendants of Scottish, English, and French Huguenot immigrants who settled in the seventeenth and eighteenth centuries during the period of English control. When Ireland received home rule in 1920 the Ulster counties remained united with Great Britain. The twenty-six more southerly counties ultimately became the independent Republic of Ireland.

The majority in the north, the so-called Unionists or Orangemen, are Protestant and fear being absorbed by the Catholic Republic of Ireland. They are determined to retain their tie with Britain. On the other hand, a Catholic minority in the north and most of the population in the Irish Republic are determined to end what they consider to be an unnatural and degrading relationship of part of their motherland with an alien power. Aggravated by religious differences as well as political loyalties, emotions at times have flared into violence. Intermittent terrorist activities against Northern Ireland have been carried out by the illegal Irish Republican Army (I.R.A.), whose members have crossed the border, bombed police stations, destroyed communications, and shot people from ambush. The I.R.A. has also carried out terrorist activities in England itself. The Irish Republican Government, while opposing this use of violence, nevertheless supports the ultimate aim of Irish unification. Meanwhile, in this sad situation prejudice and antagonism continue to smolder and occasionally flame into violence. In October 1964, there was fierce rioting in Ulster's largest city, Belfast, over the question of unifying Ireland.

Other failures to maintain existing group unities or to establish new and desirable intergroup organizations can also be cited. Like Ireland, Palestine was a diminutive state and relatively poor. Antagonisms between its two peoples, the Jews and Arabs, led first to its partition in 1947 and to war in 1948-1949 between the new nation of Israel and the Arab states of the Middle East. Victory went to Israel, but no satisfactory peace has been achieved, only an uneasy armistice. The inability of the Jews and Arabs in Palestine to resolve their differences has led to much human misery, especially for the hundreds of thousands of Palestinian Arabs who have been displaced by the war. Economic development in the Middle East has been hindered because money has been channeled into an Israeli-Arab arms race which erupted into war in 1958 and threatens to do so again. Jerusalem, a Holy City for three great religions, endures as a constant rebuke to modern man's inability to resolve differences standing in the way of wider cooperation. Indeed, in 1965, there were threats, and counter threats, to divert the life-giving waters of the Jordan to one side or the other—which, if carried out, could again plunge that unhappy region into full-scale conflict.

Failure in the West Indies

In another part of the globe, the Caribbean, it has been recognized that the numerous small islands comprising the British West Indies—such as Jamaica, Grenada, and Barbados—would profit by some form of closer union. It has been felt that political and economic integration would improve communication, increase interisland trade, and provide more efficient government services. The ten separate island governments engaged in a costly duplication of effort. The smaller islands also were fearful that, as diminutive and isolated units, they would never achieve full independence. After considerable discussion and study, the Federation of the West Indies was established in 1958. Much was expected from this accomplishment. The new union was better equipped than the individual islands to undertake a new offensive against such problems as over-population, exhausted soil, inadequate research development, and the shortage of capital with which to develop new sources of income, especially tourism. But the Federation foundered, mainly because of interisland jealousy and insular nationalism. Both Jamaica and Trinidad (the latter joined with Tobago) withdrew from the union and were granted independence by

England as two sovereign states in 1962. The Federation was officially dissolved in 1962 by act of the British Parliament. Fragmentation had triumphed over integration. A Trinidad journalist, commenting on this failure, wrote: "Our sins . . . are not of the Territories, but of our leaders, whose political ambitions, despite their protestations, are still rooted in insular rather than regional achievements."[1]

India Divided

Another example of retrograde fragmentation contrary to the impelling logic for larger regional cooperation was the partition of India in 1947. Ever since the early 1920's, this British colonial dependency, under the leadership of Mohandas K. Gandhi, the "Mahatma" (Great Soul) of the Indian people, had been seeking independence. In the late 1930's, when it became evident that British control would soon end, latent historic rivalries between the Hindu majority and Muslim minority were rekindled. The latter, under the leadership of Muhammad Ali Jinnah, were not willing to remain in an independent India controlled by a Hindu majority. After fruitless negotiations in which Britain endeavored to ensure the unity of India, the subcontinent was partitioned into two new states: India and Pakistan. Partition was a violation of the facts of geography, defensive strategy, and sound economics. Pakistan is a political incongruity consisting of two geographically distinct parts separated by approximately one thousand miles of Indian territory.

The fragmentation of the subcontinent had a dismal aftermath. An outbreak of fanatical religious rioting in both of these new nations immediately following partition cost thousands of lives. Relations between India and Pakistan—continuously strained—have included armed clashes over the disputed territory of Kashmir. In the realm of power politics, the logical need is for both nations to stand as one in defense of a common interest—the northern frontiers. Instead, continued antagonism between the two states has enabled Communist China to take advange of the feud. The festering quarrel has also meant costly expenditures on arms at a time when capital outlays for economic development are essential. Indian partition must be regarded as one of the cardinal tragedies of the twentieth century.

Cyprus and Quebec: Case Studies of Nationalism

During 1964 two examples of nationalism occupied world attention: Cyprus and Quebec. The former, a small island republic in the eastern Mediterranean, has a population of approximately 600,000 people of Greek and Turkish origin, in which the Greek Cypriots outnumber the Turks by a little more than four to one. Cyprus has been ruled by many conquerors. From 1878 to 1959, it was under British control. During this last regime its two ethnic communities lived in reasonable harmony; but each had its own educational system, distinctive language, and religion. This cultural separation was symbolized by the differences between the tall minaret of the mosque and the rounded dome of the Greek Orthodox Church. The rise of nationalism following World War II created grave rivalries between the two communities. The Greeks, led by Archbishop Makarios, wanted either *enosis* (union) with Greece or complete Cypriot independence. They insisted upon an unfettered right of self-determination. The Turkish minority countered with a demand for guarantees of protection. In 1959, London granted independence to the island but retained an armed base. Agreements were signed by which the Turks were given more power than their mere numbers warranted: a veto over defense and foreign policy, special powers relating to finance, and a guaranteed precentage of posts in the police, army, and civil service.

The Greek leaders, claiming that the Turkish minority had been obstructing government action, were determined to revise the constitution and attain unchecked majority rule. Naturally, the Turks were adamantly opposed. Bitterness increased and fighting broke out in December 1963; it continued during much of the year and took a heavy toll in lives. This bitter dispute brought Greece and Turkey to the brink of war. The U.S.S.R. took advantage of the quarrel by promising protection to the Greek Cypriots. Even NATO was threatened, for Greece and Turkey are both members. Great Britain and the United States tried fruitlessly to resolve the quarrel. In March 1964 a United Nations peace-keeping contingent was sent to Cyprus. No basic solution is yet in sight. An uneasy truce prevails. Meanwhile, the general welfare of the island's inhabitants is threatened, for economic life is nearly at a standstill.

As a result of the French and Indian War, French Quebec in 1763 became a British territory. About a century later—in 1867—Quebec was made a province in a self-governing Canadian federation. In this political union the French were given certain rights guaranteeing their religion, civil law, and language.

Until about two decades ago, Quebec remained largely rural and evinced little interest in commerce. Since World War II, however, significant social and economic changes have begun to transform the province. Major industrial development and exploitation of the region's natural resources have ensued. Cities have grown rapidly, and a dynamic cultural reawakening has occurred. An important intellectual elite has emerged determined to transform conservative and static French Quebec into a modern society. In order to achieve this, they have set out to lessen the traditional hold of the clergy, modernize the educational system, and eliminate corrupt politicians from the provincial government. Perhaps the most important objective has been to reaffirm the importance of what today is commonly referred to as the "French fact" in Canadian society, namely, the use of the French language, and the French-Canadian contribution and "style" in the arts and literature. Closely associated with these aims has been the determination in the financial field to lessen the power of English-Canadian and American capital in Quebec. They have resolved as well to reduce the felt danger of being assimilated by English-speaking North America. These aims have been held by some six million French-Canadians out of Canada's total population of twenty million.

While Canadians of French origin live in the country's various provinces, the great majority are in Quebec. In this province there is wide dissatisfaction with the status of French-speaking people in Canada. It is claimed that ever since confederation in 1867 they have been the object of discrimination. Even though bilingualism and other rights are guaranteed to the minority of English descent in Quebec, such privileges are not enjoyed by the Canadians of French ancestry living in the other provinces. In the business world and in government service the French-Canadians contend that they do not receive their fair share of positions. While the country is officially bilingual, moreover, the federal government operates mainly in English.

Since 1960, French-Canadian nationalism has grown rapidly and with it a demand by some vocal elements that Quebec be given its independence. While some degree of nationalism exists throughout Quebec, there is a small intransigent group composed mainly of the younger high-school and college generation who insist on separation and independence for their *patrie*, Quebec. *Le Rassemblement pour l'Independence Nationale*, the R.I.N. Party, represents their point of view, particularly when it speaks of the "English conquest." On occasion these extreme nationalists have resorted to terrorism, as exemplified by serious outbreaks of violence in 1963. With weapons they stole from armories, they committed acts of sabotage similar to those of the former French underground in Algeria. In the fall of 1964 they greeted Great Britain's Queen Elizabeth in Quebec with shouts of "Quebec Libre."

The startling resurgence of this French-Canadian nationalism has endangered Canadian national unity. While it is clear that in the past this national minority has been patronized and discriminated against, it is also true that some of the backwardness and second-class status has been attributable to the French-Canadians themselves. Their educational system, for example, with its emphasis upon the classics and the training of clerics, lawyers, and notaries, has not turned out adequate numbers of engineers, scientists, and future business executives.

There are signs that the majority of Canadians realize the situation is a serious threat to Canadian unity, which they want to preserve. The break-up of the Confederation would be politically and economically calamitous. Canada's Prime Minister, Lester B. Pearson, led a successful fight in Parliament to adopt a new Canadian flag, a red maple leaf on a white field with heavy red bars on either side, replacing the Red Ensign with its Union Jack in the upper left-hand corner. This change, it was hoped, would serve as a new symbol of reconciliation between the Canadians of French and British descent.

The capable and moderate French premier of Quebec, Jean Lesage, has stated that the French-Canadians ". . . are ready to accept the problems and difficulties of coexistence." Stressing that separation for his province is no solution, he insists, nevertheless, upon a new deal for Quebec which would include equality for the French in all phases of the federal government, teaching the French language to the French minorities outside Quebec, and a measure of decentralization in government (to give Quebec more control over its own affairs). Substantial concessions will have to be made by both sides if an acceptable solution is to be reached. A national election held in 1965 indicated that Quebec's voters were inclined to look for a resolution of their problems within the framework and policies of the major parties rather than support extremist groups.

Manifestations of Widening Loyalties

Notwithstanding the many instances of narrow group and national rivalries and antagonisms, there is also evidence that mankind is groping unsteadily and painfully toward more supranational unity and cooperation. Witness the Commonwealth, successor to the British Empire, which now consists of eighteen members—five white, nine African, and four Asian. This multiracial organization is unique in world history. Its members retain complete sovereignty; there is little or no provision for common action in world affairs. Yet the Commonwealth does offer a valuable opportunity for the exchange of views and discussion on matters affecting people all over the world.

Other examples of regional cooperation, even if only military, are the North Atlantic Treaty Organization (NATO) for the defense of Western Europe and the Southeast Asian Treaty Organization (SEATO) intended to defend southeast Asia. The Organization of American States (OAS) is an outstanding case of inter-American cooperation in the Western Hemisphere. As the impelling need for these groups lessens, however, the sense of group unity decreases. This is especially true now in the case of NATO which, because of French pressure, is likely to be reorganized soon.

Since 1945 the world's economic problems have increasingly been recognized as the business of all nations. The wealthy nations have accepted the responsibility of assisting those which are economically underdeveloped. Accordingly, billions of dollars have been donated or loaned in this endeavor. Still another example of widening cooperation between the peoples of the world is the American Peace Corps. The United States, the pioneer in this field, has enrolled more than 12,000 workers, and already 22 other nations have entered the same endeavor. One of the most important is West Germany, whose Development Service recruits at the rate of 1000 yearly for work overseas.

In the 1960's there have been other significant indications of widening regional cooperation or at least a growing awareness of the desirability of such action. Despite widespread political instability in the Middle East and rivalries between leaders, there is evidence of a mounting realization among the ninety million people of the Arab world of the need for more unity. The achievement of this goal could mean greater Arab prestige, accelerated economic advance, and increased political stability. A new world power would exist, extending from the Atlantic to the Persian Gulf. Egypt's President Nasser has been the pragmatic driving force behind Pan-Arabism. Lasting Arab unity must develop from the bottom up and not be imposed from above. The formation of the Arab League in 1945, the brief union of Egypt and Syria (1958-1961), and the first Arab summit meeting, in 1964, are all symptomatic of a movement toward Arab unity, but the route will be long and tortuous. Islam has been thought of as the most promising potential unifying force. It would seem, however, that the centripetal influence of religion is not as strong as the divisive forces of regional loyalties and the conflicting ambitions of rival leaders. At present the principal forces binding the Arab world together are suspicion of the West for past colonial excesses and antagonism toward Israel. More positive unifying ties are needed.

In some ways similar to Pan-Arabism is the movement for African unity. In this endeavor Kwame Nkrumah, President of Ghana, occupies a role much like that of Nasser. Nkrumah insists upon immediate action. But Africa has some eight hundred basic indigenous groups, and tribal antagonisms are numerous. The Republic of the Congo (formerly the Belgian Congo) stands as a tragic warning to those who picture the task of African unity as a simple one. A promising sign, however, was the meeting of thirty African states in Addis Ababa, Ethiopia, in 1963, at which agreement was reached on a Charter of Organization for African Unity.

Perhaps the most significant example of the waning of nationalism and the creation of a new and exciting supranational cooperative institution has been the Common Market in Western Europe. By the Treaty of Rome (1958) creating the European Economic Community, six nations—France, Western Germany, Italy, Luxembourg, Belgium, and the Netherlands—pledged to achieve economic cooperation by lowering the old national barriers to the natural flow of goods, capital, and labor. The success of this undertaking has been astounding. The economic area of the "Six" has substantially surpassed—at least temporarily—the economic growth rate of the United States. Rising standards of living have revolutionized the status of the masses. The bicycle, long a symbol of transportation, has been displaced by the automobile. The area of the "Six" could also logically be expanded to include Great Britain and countries in Scandinavia. Economic union might lead to a form of political integration; indeed, a United States of Europe is held out by some as a goal. If Western Europe were to become fully united, it could, with its population (350 million), wealth, and industrial power, become the strongest political-economic unit in the world. Such an accomplishment, and the demonstration of the advantages of regional integration, could encourage similar developments in other areas.

History shows that nationalism was once a vehicle and manifestation of progress in human affairs. Increasingly, however, the contemporary world scene indicates that international cooperation in the political, scientific, and economic spheres is desirable and in some cases even urgent. Such cooperation is growing, even though disturbing examples of divisive rivalries and loyalties remain.

Topics for Discussion:

1. Do you believe one leader and nation, such as Nasser and Egypt, can impose unity on the Middle East as Bismarck and Prussia did on Germany? How are the two situations similar and how do they differ?
2. While greater interregional and interstate cooperation seem desirable, what positive contributions and values can nationalism continue to offer in the modern world?
3. What case can be made for the thesis that Indian partition was inevitable and unavoidable? Should India and Pakistan reunite? What chance do you think there is of this happening?
4. What positive steps could be taken in Canada to reduce nationalistic controversy and prevent the secession of Quebec? Do you believe Quebec could exist as an independent nation?
5. Why is the Graeco-Turkish quarrel over Cyprus so menacing to world peace? Discuss the nature of the dispute and what alternative solutions exist. How would your outlook toward the quarrel differ if you were (1) a Greek Cypriot, (2) a Turkish Cypriot?
6. At a time when African nations are so beset with their own domestic problems, what purpose is served by discussing Pan-Africanism? In this connection, what would seem to be the strongest binding and driving force at present behind Pan-Africanism?
7. Evaluate the British Commonwealth as an experiment in international racial and political cooperation. How would you compare its role and importance with such other supranational organizations as the United Nations?
8. Does the immense disparity in national revenues (from oil) between the various Arab states pose an obstacle to unity in the Middle East? What other obstacles exist?
9. Recalling the precedent of the Zollverein and German unity, would it seem that the Common Market is an important step toward a united Europe? Discuss this statement.

3

The Politics of New Nations:

THE EROSION OF WESTERN DEMOCRACY

High Expectations of the New Nations

Since 1945, more than 65 new states have joined the family of nations. The appearance of these heirs of Western colonialism has radically changed the political map of the world, especially in Africa, the Middle East, and Asia. They vary in size from India, Pakistan, and Indonesia, to miniscule Lebanon, Rwanda, and Kuwait. All, however, have shared the legacy—created during the intense and emotional nationalistic drive for independence—of oversimplifying their problems and of too often attributing them to the evils of foreign rule. Freedom has been sought and justified on the grounds of democratic rights (such as manhood suffrage, freedom from arbitrary arrest, and freedom of speech) and self-determination. It is understandable, therefore, that practically all the new states have begun with parliamentary, liberal governments patterned after Western models.

This overly optimistic attitude toward the privileges and responsibilities which accompany the acquisition of sovereignty has not endured long among the emerging nations. Economic problems have appeared to be almost insuperable and have been complicated by a high rate of population increase. In some cases there had been inadequate political tutelage and preparation for independence by the former colonial administrations. Tribal rivalries and civil wars have weakened and frustrated some of the new governments. Political stability has been the exception, and nearly everywhere parliamentary governments have been superseded by military dictators or by authoritarian one-party systems. In one year—1958— generals took over in six countries: Iraq, Lebanon, the Sudan, Pakistan, Burma, and Thailand. Often the outward forms of parliamentary government have been retained, but these have only camouflaged centralized control. In most of the new states where effective Western parliamentary government has been shelved, a charismatic leader—a magnetic and forceful personality with mass appeal and support—has become the head of the state, either as an outright dictator or as the representative and voice of the dominant, and usually unopposed, political party. Thus Gamal Abdel Nasser has come to dominate affairs in Egypt, Julius Nyerere in Tanganyika (which joined with Zanzibar to form the state of Tanzania), Kwame Nkrumah in Ghana, Ayub Khan in Pakistan, Achmed Sukarno in Indonesia, Sékou Touré in Guinea, and Hastings Banda in Malawi.

Democracy's Decline in Asia

A survey of the political fortunes of the new Asian states will help in understanding the reasons for the erosion of Western democracy. Burma began its independence with the assassination of its prime minister and six of his colleagues. The country has since been plagued with minority revolts, stormy politics, and economic reverses. Ballot-box democracy has failed because the masses have little understanding of its forms and functions. Army leaders assumed authority, first in 1958, and again in 1962. Rule by the dictatorial Revolutionary Council continues to be the lot of the Burmese, approximately 1300 of whom have been languishing in jail as political prisoners.

The history of democracy in Pakistan has been equally discouraging. In the first eleven years of independence Pakistan had eight governments. Parliaments were ineffectual, the peasants continued to be exploited by a feudal landlord class, and political parties engaged in bitter and debilitating partisan squabbles. Declaring that the British model of government was unworkable, General Ayub Khan seized power in 1958 and has held it ever since.

Until the mid-1950's the prosperous former British island colony of Ceylon appeared to be an exception to the general failure of Western democratic forms in Asia. But after 1956 the rise of an ultranationalist movement created serious internal strains. Riots and angry clashes took place between Singhalese extremists and the Tamils, a persecuted racial minority of Indian origin. The prime minister was assassinated in 1959. The Ceylonese government was both repressive and inefficient, and in

1962 a group of high army and police officials tried unsuccessfully to seize power. In 1965 a general election brought to power a new prime minister, Dudley Senanayake, a moderate pro-Western leader intent upon undoing years of corruption, misrule, and nationalization of industry.

The former French colonial area of Indochina has since 1945 been a tragic scene of bloody revolutions. Only Cambodia, under its premier, Prince Norodom Sihanouk, has enjoyed any peace and stability. Laos has been convulsed by factionalism and the rise and fall of various regimes involved in the Cold War rivalry between the United States and the Communists. For the present, the right wing and neutralist segments have joined forces under Premier Souvanna Phouma against the Communist Pathet Lao.

In South Vietnam, the peasants have been caught in the murderous crossfire of the struggle between their unstable government at Saigon (supported by the United States) and the Communist Vietcong guerrillas (supported by North Vietnam, China, and the U.S.S.R.). From 1954 to 1963, South Vietnam achieved some stability—but at a price. Under the stern rule of President Ngo Dinh Diem the country had a government characterized by corruption, religious persecution against the Buddhists, and favoritism to a small clique of Diem's relatives. President Diem's fall and assassination in November 1963 has brought little improvement. Military coups have persisted, the Communist menace has mounted, and parliamentary government has continued to exhibit an *opéra bouffe* quality. In a concerted effort to keep the nation from falling to the Vietcong rebels (who control two thirds of South Vietnam), the United States has increased its aid program, sent substantial numbers of additional American troops (who now total 150,000 and may even double), and undertaken intensive bombing raids in both South and North Vietnam.

Western political institutions have proved equally unsuccessful in Indonesia. By 1959 its charismatic leader, Achmed Sukarno, had repudiated them. Among the new Asian states, only India, Malaysia, and the Philippines have held fast to their espoused Western democratic ideals. Yet even among this small group there has been cause for alarm. Malaysia has faced more frequent and intense attacks from Indonesia, as well as demands from the Philippines for some of its territory in Borneo. As a result of Indonesian infiltration and unfulfilled promises of economic reform, the Philippines has renewed guerrilla activities with which to deal.

The course of politics in the Middle East has differed little from that in Asia. Political instability has been endemic and marked by revolts, assassinations, and seemingly continuous conspiracy. In Syria, revolts toppled eight governments in fourteen years. Even where the outward forms of parliamentary government have existed, they have had little meaning. Arab North Africa witnessed a successful revolution in 1952 when Egypt sent its parasitic King Farouk into exile. The new government, which soon come under the control of Gamal Nasser, has been run by a military junta ostensibly working for the people's interests but without soliciting their advice. Elsewhere in North Africa the new regimes which followed the end of French rule have been authoritarian. Morocco and Libya are monarchies; and Algeria under Premier Ahmed Ben Bella's successor, Colonel Houari Boumedienne, and Tunisia under President Habib Bourguiba are "republics" in which all power rests in one party and its leaders.

One-Party States in Africa

Democratic forms have given way in Asia to military dictatorship, while in sub-Saharan Africa they have been replaced by the emergence of the one-party state. In former French Africa south of the Sahara, each nation is controlled by a single party under a leader whose charismatic qualities are glorified and personalized for the common people (usually illiterate) by such devices as his likeness on stamps and statues, and his name on new bridges and historic city squares. Organized opposition to government policy is not tolerated, and various types of authoritarian acts guarantee the continuance of the government in power and the absence of "obstruction" to its program. One can cite instances of preventive detention, manipulation of electoral laws, curbs on trade unions and student associations, and the outlawry of rival parties. In the former British African colonies, with the notable exception of Nigeria, the trend has also been to the one-party state, of which Ghana is an outstanding example.

Obstacles to Democracy in Afro-Asia

There have been some unusual factors that would have created serious problems for any new nation regardless of conditions favoring democratic government. In Indonesia, Burma, and Algeria, especially, the legacies of war have included destruction, hatred, and violence. Indochina had endured a long, demoralizing, and disruptive war against French colonialism. In South Vietnam whatever prospects remained for the achievement of a stable liberal government have been destroyed by Communist aggression and the political ambitions of the nation's military men. But even if such untoward circumstances had not been present, other basic reasons have existed for the general failure of democratic parliamentary government in the Afro-Asian World.

The crux of the problem is that a foreign form of government was imposed on societies utterly unprepared by experience (or by their indigenous institutions) to understand Western political practices. In the West, democratic government had usually taken a long time to grow; even the right to vote developed only gradually there among the masses. In the new Afro-Asian states just the small, educated, Western-oriented class has favored ballot-box democracy. Traditionally, their peoples have regarded government as remote and authoritarian. The vast majorities have been interested primarily in better social and economic conditions; the form of government, if reasonably benevolent, has mattered little. Furthermore, it is generally agreed that democracy can function satisfactorily only when most of the following conditions exist: a high degree of literacy, reasonably good standards of living, a strong middle class, an adequate cadre of efficient and dedicated civil servants, and some experience in the art of self-government. Such desiderata have not existed in the majority of emergent Afro-Asian states.

The "Apologia" for the New Authoritarianism

What is significant is not only the demise of popular representative government in most of the new nations but also the formulation of a new ideology created to justify this action. Authoritarianism exists in almost all the emergent nations. Yet a new terminology has been invented that enables Sukarno to speak of his "Guided Democracy," Nasser of his "Popular Democracy," Ayub Khan of "Basic Democracy," and the African leaders to refer proudly to their "One-Party Democracy." This new nomenclature is difficult to understand, and one critic has referred to it as "Murkophrenia." But in order to comprehend these new adaptations of democracy, it is essential to follow the arguments of its creators and defenders. In Indonesia, Sukarno proclaimed:

I have finally come to the conclusion that the cause [of political instability] lies in practicing a system not suited to our specific requirements, in our indiscriminate adoption of every feature of the system that is known as Western democracy. . . . The principles of Western democracy . . . incorporate the concept of an active opposition. . . . By accepting this concept we have come to think in a manner that is alien to the Indonesian way of life [where decisions were traditionally arrived at by consensus].[1]

Some Africans assert that beneath its "idealistic" exterior, every political party in the Western democratic nations actually represents a definite class or economic interest which it must defend. The result, in their opinion, is a squabbling among groups that has nothing in common with the interest of the nation. Proceeding from this criticism, spokesmen for the new regimes vigorously maintain that their governments are basically democratic in spirit. Pakistanis who support Ayub Khan insist that the essential element in any democracy is consent, and that any regime which enjoys mass support must be regarded as democratic. In Egypt, where Nasser claims that his military rule is democratic, it has been argued that the key to his concept of democracy is not so much the element of choice between candidates in elections as it is popular satisfaction with the individuals running the government and mass participation in implementing its progress. Sukarno explains that "Guided Democracy" is rule by a government elite which functions without a representative parliament and seeks, through discussion, to resolve different points of view.

Sub-Saharan Africa is *par excellence* the area of the one-party state. A distinctive ideology has been developed to explain and defend what those states call democracy. Protagonists of this point of view argue that democracy can exist without Western parliamentary institutions, especially without an institutionalized opposition. They believe the basic characteristic of democracy is *discussion*, and that this quality operates in their one-party systems. The essence of democracy (if not the Western forms) has always existed in tribal Africa, they contend. Within this indigenous unit, policy traditionally has been arrived at by full and continuous discussion until a consensus has been reached. All members of the tribe then accepted the agreement. This traditional practice has now been made part of the African one-party state which rests upon the consent of the people and which dispenses with an organized opposition.

One of the most moderate and wise of the new African leaders is Julius Nyerere, President of Tanzania, who has presented a cogent defense of his one-party nation (of which Tanganyika is the dominant part). Pointing out that Western nations form coalition governments in time of emergency—especially war—he argues that the African states are now in a state of national crisis which permits no differences but demands the maximum effort, for only in this way can grave problems of national unity, mass illiteracy, and economic underdevelopment be surmounted. Dismissing the need for a multiparty system, Nyerere believes that government by discussion can be achieved in his one-party structure and that there is no necessity to organize an opposition group.

While considerable criticism has been levelled against political developments in Africa, the majority of American political scientists interested in African politics tend to justify the development of one-party states and rationalize their authoritarianism. These scholars stress the continuance of considerable political debate within the dominant party. While African governments differ from the Western two- or multiparty system, they also differ from one-party regimes in Fascist and Communist states. Despite misgivings about the new African governments, some argue that the only choice is between this and political fragmentation, excessive partisan opposition, and eventual anarchy.

Balance Sheet of the One-Party Regimes

The various supporters of the one-party system have indeed been eloquent. There is, however, disturbing evidence that their arguments are frequently not supported by the facts. In order to be benevolent, the one-party state (especially the military dictatorship) requires wisdom and restraint on the part of those in power. A dominant party must allow—as its supporters have contended—for some diversity within unity. Such moderation and wisdom have not been sufficiently evident. In the one-party regimes in former French West Africa there has been considerable unrest. The absence of satisfactory institutional channels for the expression of political opposition has already resulted in plots to overthrow existing regimes, often through purges and violence; in response, those in power have tightened their controls. Under such conditions more plots seem imminent.

It is still premature to predict the direction of one-party regimes in most of former British Africa: Kenya, Uganda, Zambia, and Malawi. Tanzania, however, does seem to have the kind of one-party government envisaged by its supporters. Under President Nyerere there is a single party, but considerable discussion of issues is permitted within the party structure. The press is not muzzled, and the civil rights of the individual are generally respected.

The ominous potentialities inherent in one-party rule have been exemplified in Ghana, formerly the British colony of the Gold Coast and the first African nation to gain its independence. Its leader, Kwame Nkrumah, in 1957 was the idol of African nationalists; and his newly freed country was the symbol of liberalism and democracy for emergent Africa. But almost immediately, Nkrumah began to muzzle the press and all opposition—even within his own party. By 1964, Ghana's parliament had become a rubber stamp. Only one party is legal, the judiciary has been rendered impotent, and many of the old colleagues of Nkrumah are either in exile or in prison. An outright dictator has developed in the classic mold. His presence has been idealized by a controlled press and radio, and he has been presented to his people as the Great Redeemer and His Messianic Majesty. The response against Nkrumah also has been classic. Attempts have been made to assassinate him. As a result he has tended to isolate himself in a massive castle left by the former colonial regime.

The Middle Eastern nations exhibit no particular pattern of politics in their so-called parliamentary systems except instability; coups and revolutions have occurred with monotonous regularity. Egypt is an exception under the benevolent, reformist control of Colonel Nasser, who has pushed forward badly needed land reforms, mass education, industrialization, and irrigation (the Aswan High Dam). An intelligent overall evaluation of this military dictatorship cannot be made now, as his domestic achievements may be endangered by personal ambition and adventurism in foreign affairs. The military budget totals about 300 million dollars a year. Nasser seems determined to try to crush Israel, to circumscribe drastically Western economic influence in the Arab states, and to unify the Middle East under his leadership.

Parliamentary institutions in Asia, with the notable exceptions we have mentioned (India, Malaysia, and the Philippines), have also failed. Some of the regimes are only moderately authoritarian, as exemplified by those of General Ayub Khan in Pakistan and General Ne Win in Burma.

Sukarno's Indonesia: A Case Study

Indonesia, however, might be termed the "Ghana" of southeast Asia. This nation of islands, with the fifth largest population in the world (over 100 million), has rich undeveloped natural resources. However, 15 years after its independence, Indonesia has reached a hazardous state. Declining exports, food shortages, and rampant inflation have brought it to the verge of bankruptcy. Its population problem has been acute; two million births have occurred each year. While there have been other causative factors —the failure of the Dutch to provide adequate higher education and appoint Indonesians to important posts, the waste and disorganization resulting from the colonial war against the Netherlands—the main responsibility for the present crisis rests, in the opinion of many observers, on Indonesia's flamboyant and charismatic President Sukarno.

Sukarno has been President of Indonesia from its independence. Upon assuming office he embarked upon a number of ruinous policies. Tremendous sums have been spent on arms, financed in large part by loans from the Soviet Union. Money was wasted on public monuments, buildings for the Asian games, and a grandiose tourist hotel. Armed revolts against his authority were triggered in the outer islands by Surkarno's excessive centralization of power in Java. He has carried out such disastrous economic policies as completely centralizing government control of the economy, seizing foreign properties (including that of American oil companies), failing to retain 50,000 Dutchmen vital to the country's business, and harassing foreign concerns which have not yet been nationalized. In 1965 the Indonesian government announced that it had taken control of all foreign-owned concerns and property. Observers concluded that this action in fact represented outright confiscation.

This unstable situation has permitted little chance to build effective parliamentary government. Cabinets proved corrupt and inefficient. Indonesia had 50 political parties in the early 1950's. Then in 1958 Sukarno began to initiate his program of "Guided Democracy," and a number of purely consultative bodies of questionable usefulness were set up. In 1964, with the support of the army, he became the absolute ruler for life as both president and prime minister. All opposition parties which did not support his rule were banned.

Amidst all the problems of a swiftly deteriorating economy, Sukarno's only solution has been to keep the masses in a continuous state of emotional nationalism. He has mesmerized his huge audiences with a torrent of slogans and phrases and employed the technique of "the whipping boy." First came the quarrel with the Dutch over possession of their colonial territory of West New Guinea; more recently President Sukarno has announced his intention to use force to break up the Federation of Malaysia. Ironically he has achieved part of his goal not through force but because of a power struggle between the Chinese in Singapore and the

Malays, as a result of which Malaysia reluctantly expelled Singapore from the Federation. His prophecy for the rest of Malaysia remains uncertain, but there are numerous indications that Indonesia faces mounting economic privation. An abortive coup in 1965 set off a bloody power struggle between Indonesia's Communist party and the military. The ailing Sukarno seemed unable to halt the civil strife.

The virtual collapse of the Western parliamentary system among the new nations of the world constitutes one of the most significant occurrences in the twentieth century. It is evident that Western political theory and governmental forms are alien to the basic traditions of these lands and are considered inappropriate to meet the urgent socioeconomic conditions of underdevelopment. For the foreseeable future, the logical type of government for most of Afro-Asia is some variant form midway between the liberal, Western two- or multiparty system and the totalitarian Communist or Fascist regimes. Such a compromise, however, must provide for some consideration of the basic freedoms of the individual, ensure stability, and protect the masses from exploitation. Within a more authoritarian framework than most Western citizens desire, a few of the new governments are doing just this. But in others the leader or the party is veering more and more toward outright dictatorship. If such practice continues to spread, not only will parliamentary democracy have failed in Afro-Asia but its successor will also share the same fate.

Topics for Discussion:

1. Compare President Nyerere of Tanzania and his government with that of President Sukarno in Indonesia. To what extent do you think the differences between the two governments stem from the personalities involved rather than from the problems of each nation?
2. Discuss whether the recent history of the emerging nations strongly suggests that the form of government best suited for them for a substantial period would be benevolent authoritarianism.
3. How many of the tests, given in this chapter, for the successful functioning of democracy exist anywhere in the Afro-Asian world?
4. Evaluate the defense given by African leaders for their one-party governments.
5. Discuss the ominous potentialities inherent in such authoritarian regimes as that of Ghana.
6. "The naive hopes and faith in democracy as a pervasive world movement, such as existed in the early years of this century, have been completely refuted. In the 1960's democracy, Western style, definitely has become a world minority movement." Comment on this statement.
7. If a nation provides no institutional channel for the expression of political opposition, how justified is the opposition in attempting to overthrow the existing government in order to provide such a channel?

4

Societal Wrongs and Human Rights

Discrimination Against Minorities

In nearly all societies there exist minority groups set off from the rest of the population because of their racial, economic, or cultural distinctiveness. One calls to mind the Muslim minority in India or the Hindu community in Pakistan. Other examples that could be cited are the Greeks in Turkey, the Coptic Christians in Egypt, the Indians in Burma, and the Chinese in Indonesia. The United States has various minority groups, such as the Negroes, Jews, Puerto Ricans, and Mexicans. And since World War II, England has experienced a large influx of Commonwealth immigrants from the British West Indies, India, and Pakistan. One of the contemporary world's most urgent problems is how best to secure equal treatment for all peoples in plural societies (those in which there are several different cultural or racial groups) regardless of their race, religion, or economic status.

History provides many examples of discrimination by dominant elements in society against groups considered inferior, dangerous, unimportant, or just "different." One recalls the servile status of the medieval serf exploited by the landed nobility, the disabilities imposed on Catholics in the British Isles—especially those in Ireland—following the Reformation; and those restrictions placed upon the Protestant Huguenot minority in Catholic France. During the heyday of the Turkish Ottoman Empire, the Sultan's Christian subjects, the despised "Rayahs," were treated badly; and in India intolerable burdens were placed on the Hindu peoples by the ruling Muslims. History offers many examples of man's inhumanity to man.

Since World War I increasing attention has been paid to rectifying this type of discrimination. The barbarities practiced by the Nazis against the Jews during the 1930's and 1940's gave further impetus to this movement. Following the Second World War the Charter of the United Nations reaffirmed faith in the fundamental rights of all human beings. This belief was given concrete form in 1948 when the General Assembly approved the much-debated Universal Declaration of Human Rights. This pronouncement bespoke aspirations rather than immediate actualities, for many of its provisions could not possibly be implemented throughout the world in the near future. It expressed such ideal sentiments as "All human beings are born free and equal in human dignity and rights."

Throughout the contemporary world numerous examples of the denial of basic human rights still exist. Three of the most significant and complex are the caste system in India, the practice of *apartheid* in the Republic of South Africa, and the struggle for civil rights by the Negro in the United States. While all three are in some way alike, other wide differences make each unusual.

India: The Caste System

Hindu India has a unique way of life in which all social groups are hierarchically graded and divided. All orthodox Hindus belong to a caste group by reason of birth in which they must stay as long as they want to remain Hindus. The origin of the system is unclear, but traditionally there have been four basic orders or castes: the Brahmans, the priests and scholars; the Kshatriyas, the warriors and rulers; the Vaishyas, the merchants; and the Shudras, the workers and peasants. Beneath and outside the accepted hierarchy have been the despised outcastes or untouchables. Today there are more than 3,000 distinct castes, each socially separate, and insulated by various taboos and prohibitions. Members of a particular caste, for example, do not marry outside their group (endogamy) and will not eat with members of other castes.

While certain discriminatory practices exist between the upper castes, it is the untouchables who have labored under the grossest injustices. Hindu custom in the past has prohibited them from entering temples, from using certain streets, and from attending public schools. They have been forced to live in designated areas, separated from the other caste Hindus. Generally the untouchables have done the most loathsome and menial tasks and, in a land where subsistence-living and even starvation are all too common, their living standards have been the lowest. They have been shunned by other members of the community who have believed their touch or even proximity to be "polluting." The number of untouchables, reported by the 1961 census as 60 million, has undoubtedly increased.

The caste system has been repeatedly attacked through the centuries; as far back as the sixth century B.C., the Buddha denounced its excesses.

Muslim invaders brought with them the idea of the essential equality of all followers of Mohammed and succeeded in converting considerable numbers of Hindus to their faith. Under British rule the Indian courts of justice introduced the principle of equality of all men before the law; and various Hindu reform movements—the last by Gandhi—sought to purge the caste system of its worst abuses. The impact of new social attitudes from the West in recent decades has encouraged the younger educated Indians progressively to ignore the old caste taboos. The constitution of independent India sought to reconcile traditional caste custom with the modern ideas of equality and basic rights. It did not end the caste system, as some believe, but did abolish both discrimination on the grounds of caste and the practice of untouchability. A law was later passed providing penalties for such discrimination. As in other countries, legislation does not always guarantee a solution. A government report in 1953 indicated there had been no "appreciable improvement with regard to the practice of untouchability." As far as the caste system itself is concerned, there is abundant evidence that it has branched out into new fields, especially that of politics. Electioneering now revolves around caste rivalries, and the most important ingredient in state politics is that of caste. Political parties have been organized by the larger castes, and candidates are often selected on the basis of their caste membership. This situation is paradoxical for the caste system, which in some respects is a major obstacle to the leveling process of democracy, now also provides a mechanism through which democratic elections can serve the interest of the voter.

Unlike most other forms of social differentiation, the caste system is ineluctably tied in with a religion, Hinduism, and its tenets regarding the cosmic process of "salvation." Thus, a Hindu believes that his soul evolves from a primitive, ignorant state—exemplified in the Shudra caste—to one of knowledge and spiritual enlightenment—that of the Brahman. This spiritual evolution requires many births—hence the Hindu's belief in the doctrine of reincarnation. Consequently, the caste system gives meaning to a Hindu's life so that to repudiate it would be similar to a Christian giving up all hope of heavenly immortality. In the future the practice of caste will probably be modified to correspond with Western ideas of civil equality and democracy. There is, however, little chance that it will die out. Two caste customs are likely to continue as long as Hinduism: 1) the acceptance of caste status, and 2) marriage within one's own group.

South Africa's Racial Dilemma

The plural society of the Republic of South Africa is one of the most complicated in existence. In this troubled land live just over three million people of European ancestry, eleven million Bantu Africans, one and one-half million Coloreds (a racially mixed group), and a half million Asians of Indian descent. The major part of South African history has concerned the rivalry between the two dominant groups of European origin: the Afrikaners (of Dutch descent) and the English. This hostility led to the Boer War (1899-1902) and to the establishment of a new sovereign nation, the Union of South Africa, in which the Afrikaner element was dominant politically. During the 1920's and 1930's intermittent hostility arose between the two major communities of European ancestry over such issues as language, the nation's official flag, and the nature of the connection with Great Britain. The last issue disappeared when South Africa left the Commonwealth in 1961. In recent years those of European descent in South Africa have closed ranks in the face of what they regard as the growing threat to "white civilization" from the non-white majority.

Even before World War I, it was evident that the South Africans of European descent had no intention of sharing political power with the Bantu Africans, even though they planned to continue to use their much-needed labor. Native reserves were set aside in 1913, and no Bantu African was permitted to leave without special permission. When not in these areas, the Africans working for Caucasian employers were controlled by a pass system and by residential segregation. Nor could a Bantu African participate in politics outside his reserves. A color-bar reserved certain forms of work for the whites. Following the Afrikaner Nationalist party victory in the election of 1948, the government has proceeded to extend the system of racial segregation which it has called *apartheid* (separateness). A number of laws have been enacted to implement the new policy. These measures have been designed to prevent racial mixing, to ensure complete residential segregation, to provide a special curriculum for Bantu African school children, and to negate the power of African trade unions. In effect, *apartheid* means utilizing Negro labor wherever useful but keeping the Africans socially segregated and politically inarticulate.

Repression naturally has stirred opposition—both from liberal-minded South Africans of European descent and from westernized, urban, and educated non-white Africans such as Chief Albert Luthuli (Nobel Peace Prize winner in 1960). In the main, the opposition has been peaceful and nonviolent, but bloody incidents have occurred. At Sharpeville, 70 unarmed Bantu Africans were killed by police and more than 200 were wounded. Sabotage has become more frequent; in 1964 at the famous Rivonia Trial a number of Africans, including Mandela, "the Black Pimpernel," were sentenced to life imprisonment for having blown up buildings and communication lines. To curb and control the unrest, the government has enacted stringent laws empowering it to restrict free speech, to imprison people without trial for 90 days, and to regard as treason certain forms of criticism directed against the government. Sabotage has been defined as "the advocacy of any political or economic change," and conduct "embarrassing state administration."

In the first half of the 1960's *apartheid* has attracted growing world criticism. The Afro-Asian nations in particular have carried on a continuous diplomatic and press campaign against what has been labelled inhuman and abhorrent discrimination on the basis of race. The United Nations General Assembly by an overwhelming vote has condemned the repressive measure of *apartheid*. In addition, the Security Council has been asked to plan economic sanctions against the South African government. A number of nations, including the United States, have agreed not to sell arms to South Africa. An international conference was convened in London in 1964 to investigate the kind of pressures that might be invoked to secure the abolition of *apartheid*.

The bankruptcy of its policy and a growing sense of its world isolation led the South African government to make a dramatic and even revolutionary move. In 1959 the government announced its intention to make "provision for the gradual development of self-governing Bantu national units." Eight such territorial states are envisaged. Liberal economic aid has been promised to make them self-sufficient. The first state in this Bantustan program, the Transkei, was established in 1963 with a population of more than three million people. South African exponents of Bantustan argue that this program will eventually result in the establishment of an association of Bantu African nations with the Caucasian section of what is now South Africa. While the ultimate form of this association has not been spelled out precisely, it will permit each section a considerable degree of domestic self-government. However, such affairs as defense, foreign relations, and certain financial matters will remain in the hands of South Africans of European descent. A large number of Bantus will gain their livelihood in the white areas where their labor is badly needed, but they will only be able to participate in politics in the specific African area to which they belong. In the words of South Africa's Prime Minister, "If the various Bantu national units show the ability to attain the required stage of self-sufficiency, they will eventually form a South African commonwealth together with white South Africa which will serve as its core and as guardian of the emerging Bantu states."[1]

Exploiting the doctrine of self-determination, the South Africans of English and Dutch descent maintain they have the same right as the Bantus to their own nation state and this right can only be secured for both races under the program of Bantustan. Some foreign observers contend, however, that this is fallacious reasoning because the Bantu employ the argument of self-determination to oppose Bantustan in the creation of which they had no voice. The status of the Coloreds and those of Asian origin remains unclear as neither has a tribal homeland and thus will continue to live in the white areas.

The Bantustan proposals may alleviate tensions in South Africa for a time, but most authorities do not believe they can be a long-term solution. The non-Caucasian population is growing at twice the rate of that of the South Africans of European origin; and the proposed African states cannot possibly support their rapidly increasing numbers. At least 30 percent of the Bantu Africans will be forced to work and live in the Caucasian areas. This urban African potentially constitutes the most discontented element in Bantustan for he is becoming increasingly westernized and does not wish to be tied to any tribal state, no matter how self-governing. He is developing a taste for Western culture, and desires all the rights and opportunities that his contact with Europeans has brought him to value. In South Africa the only long-run solution would seem to be a biracial society in which the intrinsic worth of any individual would be measured by his ability rather than his color. Meanwhile, the politically conscious Bantu African is increasingly insisting upon "one man—one vote."

The Negro in the United States

In India the caste system has been considered divinely ordained by Hinduism, and in South Africa *apartheid* has been the official policy of the state. But in the United States an embarrassing dichotomy has existed between the prevailing practice of discrimination against the Negro and the equalitarian ideals which are central to the American way of life.

The Negro problem can only be understood in the light of American history. The institution of slavery left behind it throughout the country, but especially in the South, the tradition of a white master-Negro servant relationship and a belief in white superiority. The tragic post-Civil War Reconstruction period reinforced the desire to continue white supremacy among many Southerners. During this period Congress passed the first civil rights law and the Fourteenth and Fifteenth Amendments to insure the rights of the former slaves. The Southern states reacted to Negro emancipation by passing the "Black Codes," which regulated their economic and social life. In addition, *sub rosa* coercion and violence were utilized by such groups as the Ku Klux Klan. These types of extralegal intimidation became a tragic legacy that still plagues the nation a century later. Yet, until the 1880's large numbers of Negroes in the South actually voted and shared unsegregated facilities, held government jobs, and worked in skilled industries. But during that decade southern states began to enact a series of laws introducing segregation in all facets of life, and by means of the Poll Tax and exclusion from primaries effectively barred most Negroes from political activity.

The concept of "separate but equal" became the dominant racial philosophy and was approved by the United States Supreme Court in 1896. The decision asserted that enforced separation did not stamp Negroes "with a badge of inferiority." But while the races had always been separate, little was done to make them equal. For example, one southern state in 1915 spent 23 dollars on educating every white child and only two dollars for each Negro youngster.

Following World War I, the Supreme Court began to veer in its philosophy toward protecting and ensuring Negro rights. In the 1930's it ruled against the "separate but equal doctrine" in higher education, but not until after World War II did the climate of opinion on racial issues change significantly.

In 1948 civil rights became a national issue and has remained one. The newly independent Afro-Asian nations have championed racial equality and have reacted strongly against discrimination on the basis of color. American Negroes, influenced by this new current of opinion, have begun to manifest both a pride in their race and the determination to enjoy their constitutional rights. The Supreme Court has not been oblivious to the need for action. In 1954, in the famous case of *Oliver Brown* vs. *Board of Education, Topeka,* it ruled that in public education "separate educational facilities are inherently unequal" and called for "all deliberate speed" in school desegregation. A massive civil rights movement employing passive resistance was also initiated; the first dramatic incident was the Negro boycott of segregated local buses in Montgomery, Alabama, in 1955. Two years later federal troops were called to enforce integration of Little Rock, Arkansas' Central High School.

Since 1960, the campaign has moved more rapidly as the Negroes have employed sit-ins, wade-ins, and pray-ins. The year 1963 was crucial, for it witnessed the much publicized protest demonstrations in Birmingham, Alabama, the march on Washington in quest of a new civil rights law, and even the selection by a national magazine of Martin Luther King as Man of the Year. This champion of Negro rights gained further world recognition in 1964 when he was awarded the Nobel Peace Prize. The same year Congress passed the most comprehensive civil rights bill since the Civil War; it outlawed many forms of discrimination and empowered the federal government to take certain actions to enforce its provisions. However, even its voter registration provisions were circumvented by some southern communities. In response to this evasion of the law and the Selma, Alabama civil rights protest of 1965 (which included a "freedom march" of 54,000 demonstrators from Selma to Montgomery and the killing of a white civil rights worker), Congress passed still another law, eliminating literacy tests as a means of discrimination in national, state, or local elections. The House of Representatives also began an investigation of the resurgent Ku Klux Klan.

All in all, with the backing of stronger federal laws and a more determined federal government, desegregation has made progress in schools, public facilities, restaurants, and hotels. New job opportunities for Negroes have been opening up; gradually exclusion from unions is being rectified. More attention is being given to providing better education and job training for Negroes in order to end the old situation of "last hired and first fired."

Social change, especially when it touches race, is a difficult process. It usually is protracted and often accompanied by resistance and even violence. The enactment of federal laws and the exercise of sanctions by the state against offenders can be effective. But racial discrimination will disappear altogether only when all the people concerned cease to believe in it. It has been said that "conscience and public opinion enforce the laws, the police suppress the exceptions." The excesses of the caste system in India, the inequalities inherent in South African *apartheid,* and the obvious and the unseen discriminations operating against the American Negro can only be completely removed by the process of education, and the general growth of public enlightenment.

Topics for Discussion:

1. List as many examples as you can of the problems of discrimination and denial of human rights that exist in the world. In each case indicate the basis of prejudice: national culture, race, religion, economics, or other.
2. What basic rights are emphasized in the United Nations Declaration of Human Rights?
3. Do you support the right of the United Nations to bring pressure upon any nation to secure the end of racial discrimination? What type of action can and should be taken? Which section of the United Nations Charter justifies taking action?
4. Does the emphasis upon status in the United States imply the existence of a caste system, and if so, what is its basis?
5. Discuss the merits and defects of the Bantustan program now in effect in South Africa. Evaluate what hope its future form holds.
6. How credible is the argument of South Africans of European ancestry that just as others in the world have claimed the right to unfettered nationalism, so they also have the right to determine their destiny free of the control of the African majority in South Africa?
7. What is implied in the admonition not to be too" contemporary minded" when studying racial and other problems of discrimination? How would this statement apply to the United States?
8. Analyze and comment on this statement from the preceding chapter: "Conscience and public opinion enforce the laws, the police suppress the exceptions."

5

The Population Explosion

"Be Fruitful and Multiply"

That the major religions have traditionally sanctioned, and indeed encouraged, high fertility in human reproduction can be readily understood when we recall the severe checks upon population growth throughout virtually the entire course of mankind's planetary existence. Without cessation, famine, pestilence, and war combined to challenge men's capacities to survive, and evidence attests that for the thousands of centuries preceding our modern technological age, high birth rates were balanced almost precisely by high mortality rates.

If, as some discoveries suggest, the life-span of the human species may date back as far as 1,600,000 years, the estimated number of people inhabiting the earth during that immense span totals some 96 billion. However, only about one-third of these lived before 6000 B.C., that is, prior to the Neolithic Age. Because of a primitive technology (an estimated two square miles were required to support one person during the food-gathering stage), the planet's population had grown to only some five million by 6000 B.C. The Neolithic breakthrough to a food-producing economy radically altered the situation. From 6000 B.C. to 1650 A.D., extending through the Bronze and Iron Ages and into early modern time, some 42 billion births took place, resulting also in a hundredfold increase in planetary population (from five million to almost 500 million).

Yet, dramatic though these figures are when compared with the preceding millennia, they pale before the acceleration in births and planetary numbers in the last three centuries. Within that brief period, some 23 billion births occurred, and the earth's population increased sixfold to more than three billion in 1965. And what of the century ahead?

Each day that passes sees the world's population increase by more than 160,000 (some 61 million per year—almost one-third the population of the United States). This increase would stretch as a single-file column halfway around the equator. On the basis of present trends, moreover, the earth will have to support four billion persons by 1980, and at least six billion by the year 2000.

In other words, its population can be expected to double and, since a large proportion of the present population is undernourished, the overall food supply will have to be more than doubled. To make long-term demographic projections is hazardous because of changes in technology, in societal attitudes, and in behavior patterns. But we must also recognize that, on the basis of present trends, the earth's population will number 12 billion around 2040 A.D. True, the picture may alter radically in the decades ahead. Nevertheless, we should also note that thus far population growth has actually exceeded the high projections prepared by United Nations demographers. The world's population is now increasing at an estimated 2 percent annually (which means that it doubles every 35 years); to continue this rate of growth for the next century would result in a total population several times the largest estimate of the maximum number that could be supported by present knowledge and technology.

The problem is exacerbated by two other factors: the uneven distribution of the world's present population (two-thirds live on about 7 percent of the land area), and the differing growth rates of the major regions of the planet. According to United Nations' statistics, while all regions without exception gained between 1950 and 1960, the rate of growth varied from 7 percent for northern and Western Europe to 29 percent for Middle America. Asia, with its 21 percent, a rate slightly higher than the world average of 19 percent, is estimated to have gained 293 million people, or 60 percent of the total world increase. Birth rates average some 40 per 1000 persons in Africa, Asia, Middle America, and South America, whereas they are only slightly more than half that figure in Europe, North America, and the Soviet Union. This means that the population explosion is taking place in those areas which are technologically underdeveloped and least able to cope with the increasing imbalance between economic production and biological reproduction. It seems safe to assert that if the world can escape a thermonuclear holocaust—which would represent the most effective "solution" to all our ills—the population explosion must become *the* planetary problem during the next hundred years.

How the Explosion Occurred

Population change results from three interrelated components: mortality, fertility, and migration. Of these, the changing relations of birth and death rates have primarily determined both the overall increase in planetary population and the relative sizes of populations in different regions and countries. Unquestionably, the major cause for the spectacular jump in modern population has been the rapid fall in death rates. In the West, the agricultural and industrial revolutions of the eighteenth and early nineteenth centuries resulted in higher levels of living and, consequently, higher nutritional standards, as well as improvements in sanitation and public health. In effect, the decline in mortality rates in the West derived more from economic than medical gains, whereas the reverse has occurred in the past century, especially in non-Western regions. The most significant change that has occurred regarding mortality since the Second World War is that much of the health technology developed in the industrialized countries has now become accessible to the underdeveloped nations, whose death rates have been falling spectacularly regardless of their ability to match the gain with commensurate progress in economic development and production.

A few examples will underscore this fact. Thanks to the invention in 1940 of chlorophenothane (DDT), the eradication of malaria on a vast scale became possible. One result was that the death rate in Ceylon plummeted from 20 per 1000 in 1940 to 13 per 1000 in 1948. Again, the Muslim population in Algeria has experienced a decline in death rates from more than 30 per 1000 in 1946 to less than 15 per 1000 in 1958. Such results from the application of Western medical technology have had the effect of reducing within a decade or less the death rate by the same percentage that it required Western countries a century or more to attain prior to 1900.

This decline in mortality levels is of course reflected in the factor of life expectancy. Before 1800 the expectation of life at birth was thought to be from 25 to 40 years, but because of the application of medical science a steady increase has occurred. A United Nations' study covering 15 countries shows that between 1900 and 1950 the life expectation of men increased from 49.6 to 66.0 years, about three years per decade. In approximately the same period the decennial increase for women rose to four years. These results are rapidly becoming universal.

Meanwhile, however, birth-rates have *not* declined significantly during this same period. In the economically advanced regions, they vary from between 15 and 19 per 1000 in Western Europe to 25 per 1000 in the Soviet Union and North America. By contrast, in the underdeveloped regions the variations range from 40 per 1000 in East Asia to 48 per 1000 in tropical and southern Africa, and as high as 49 per 1000 in parts of Latin America.

It should also be noted that the decline in mortality rates and the lengthening of the life-span have the effect, too, of increasing "effective fertility." Of every 100 white females born in the United States in 1950, 97 can be expected to survive to 20 years of age, while 91 will survive to the end of the childbearing period. These figures represent more than three and eleven times, respectively, the proportions for white females who survived to these ages four centuries ago. The death rates prevailing in Guatemala in 1950, however, permit only half of the females to live to the end of the childbearing period. If and when the Guatemalan mortality rate falls to the level of the United States in 1950, the number of new-born females surviving to the end of the childbearing period would increase by 85 percent. A corresponding decrease in the birth rate would be required to prevent this increase in survivorship from resulting in a rapid acceleration in the existing rate of population growth, which is already excessive. In other words, this decrease in the death rate would require a decrease in the birth rate of more than 40 percent merely to maintain the status quo.

Traditionally, the death rate has fallen before the birth rate, resulting in a period when population increase is rapid. Consequently, the duration of the period separating the birth and death rates becomes crucial. It appears clear already that the underdeveloped countries will deviate significantly from the classical Western experience, in which death rates fell slowly and were subsequently followed by declining birth rates. In India, on the other hand, the death rate fell from 44 per 1000 in 1890 to 31 per 1000 forty years later (and has since fallen further), whereas the birth rate remained more or less constant (46 in 1890 and 45 in 1930). During the past two decades, moreover, the birth rate in underdeveloped countries has not changed appreciably. One authority forcefully contends that the combination of a medieval birth rate with a twentieth century death rate is responsible for the present high rate of population increase. With few exceptions, there is no indication that the birth rate will soon decline.

Some Consequences of the Problem

Economists compute that, in order to raise national income while population is expanding by 2 or 3 percent per annum, it is necessary to save and invest 9 percent annually, since to achieve an income increment of one unit approximately three additional units of capital are required. For the greater number of underdeveloped countries, unhappily, this rate of savings and investment is far from being achieved. The over-all, and increasingly dangerous, result is that the gap in living standards between the rich and poor nations is constantly widening. This gap stems in no small measure from four major factors in the population problem, which retard economic growth in the underdeveloped countries. They comprise, in addition to the high rate of population growth, an unfavorable age structure, unbalanced population distribution, and inadequately educated and trained manpower. We might briefly examine these factors.

One result of high fertility in underdeveloped countries is the large proportion of persons under 15 years of age—approximately 40 percent among the populations of Asia, Africa, and Latin America, in contrast to

24 percent, for example, in Sweden. This high percentage operates against economic development for at least two reasons. Because of the high proportion of children below working age, *per capita* labor and income alike are reduced. Again, a much greater proportion of the limited resources of the underdeveloped countries must be allocated to "social" rather than to "economic" investment—that is, to child-rearing, training of teachers, and the construction of schools and other facilities for the young. Moreover, savings are low or even nonexistent among large families. Traditionally, these families have subsisted in the countryside where the land can normally provide the bare necessities.

Since World War II, however, there has been a rapid—and many economists think excessive—migration to the cities which do not possess the kind of economic base to support such migratory influxes and thus cope with an accelerating rural-urban imbalance. Hence, we find in and around the proliferating urban sites throughout Asia, Africa, and Latin America, sprawling shanty-towns devoid of the basic amenities of modern existence as experienced in the West. Ironically, to the extent that large investments are allocated to streets, water supply, sewerage, and electricity in order to help provide such amenities, the amount of capital available for vitally-needed industrial expansion is in turn reduced. Without this expansion the underdeveloped countries can never hope to catch up with Western standards of living.

High population growth retards investment not only in economic but also in human resources. To try to keep pace with such growth by doubling, or even quadrupling primary school construction is laudable and indeed an indispensable requirement for the burgeoning populations of underdeveloped regions in the twentieth century; but no less indispensable is a sharp improvement in the quality of education. Unless specialized skills and higher education can be imparted to a much larger proportion of these populations than is yet the case, these countries may well remain the "drop-outs" in a world progressively geared to the increasing complexities of the technological order.

High population growth is no less far-reaching in its social implications. Rural overpopulation (where the land cannot support its people) is tied up with inequitable land distribution. In almost all underdeveloped countries, the land tenure system permits the existence both of small numbers of very large estates, *latifundia*, which are by no means always employed by their well-to-do owners for the maximum advantage of the local population, and of large numbers of very small holdings, *minifundia*, which are often too minute to enable modern agricultural techniques to be employed to improve production. Both the *latifundia* and the overfragmented *minifundia* tend to retain primitive methods of cultivation. The resultant low harvests force large numbers of the rural population to seek a new life in the cities. In some African countries, the urban population has trebled within the past 15 years, while on the continent as a whole it has doubled. In India, the city population rose between 1941 and 1951 by 39 percent, three times the national increase. Yet a recent survey revealed that the walls and roofs of only about one out of eight of the urban houses in India were made of durable materials; that 39 percent had only one room; and that only 20 percent had individual latrines. In Greater Calcutta and Bombay, over three-quarters of all families lived in one-room tenements. Such slum conditions increase social dislocation, health costs, crime, and political unrest against the government in power.

It would seem obvious that a reduction in birth rates must materially improve social conditions in the countryside and city alike. Yet there are major inhibiting factors at work. One is the traditional value attached to large families; underdeveloped societies tend to be less individualistic than those in the West and are consequently less inclined to hold with the argument that fewer children can be looked after and reared better. The centuries-old experience of high mortality rates is yet another reason why many married couples believe in numerous offspring as a form of "life insurance" for the family so that at least one or two children can grow to adulthood. Despite the spectacular success of medical technology, such attitudes die slowly, as do traditional religious beliefs, for example in Muslim countries.

Hindu *mores*, on the other hand, have tended to buttress such institutions as the joint-family and to consider control over one's self more important than a society's control over its environment. Hinduism, it might be added, does not object to the use of artificial means for curbing the birth rate. However, while contraceptives and other means of restraining fertility have been widely adopted in the West and Japan, they have made little progress thus far in the underdeveloped countries. To understand the determinants of fertility in each society requires further research on the relevant attitudes, values, and patterns of behavior.

We must also recognize that political factors can encourage continuation of the population explosion. Various societies are dominated by totalitarian regimes which extract a maximum of physical labor from their people. Again, Marxist theorists have refused to admit that overpopulation can affect socialist economies as adversely as those of the capitalists. This attitude apparently continues to motivate the Peking regime which, in addition, may be planning both to employ China's huge and rapidly growing population to "justify" territorial expansion and to obtain a human "stockpile" against possible nuclear warfare which could conceivably wipe out half a given population within a few hours.

Finally, a deep-seated feeling exists in the political sphere that the strength and prestige of a country are intimately related to the size of its population. Industrially advanced countries with high living standards can afford such views, perhaps, but many of the leaders of underdeveloped countries remain impervious to the carefully-marshalled statistics of economists who can demonstrate that failure of economic production to keep pace with biological reproduction results in a lowering of nutritional standards and a weakening of the national structure. President Sukarno comes to mind as an illustration. Although Java suffers from runaway population growth—so that it contains some 72 million people who can subsist only because the government imports hundreds of thousands of tons of rice annually—Sukarno boasts that his country of 110 million ranks fifth among the world's powers; and he anticipates a doubling of that population within a few decades. Either he has no idea of the economic and social suffering which the attainment of that figure can entail for the Indonesian masses—especially in view of present-day inflation and deterioration of the national economy—or Sukarno's political plans call for territorial expansion. Meanwhile, Indonesia continues to combine a medieval birth rate with a twentieth-century death rate.

The Situation in Latin America

Some months before his death; President Kennedy declared: "I regard Latin America as the most critical area in the world today," while Vice President Humphrey has maintained that the social structure and external policies of the nations of that region are so uncertain that Latin America should receive first priority in this country's foreign policy. The imbalance between economic production and biological reproduction helps account for the social instability and political uncertainty of this region.

The most rapid rate of population growth anywhere in the world is taking place in Middle and South America where, if present trends continue, the population will double every 26 years. By 1960, the number of inhabitants in Latin America exceeded that in North America, and by the end of the century it may be twice as large. Despite its 2.3 percent birth rate, the southern continent in 1960 possessed only 7 percent of the earth's total population; hence, given its physical size, it had a low over-all demographic density. Because of massive problems, including large-scale erosion, extensive rain-forests in its tropical areas (such as the Amazon basin), the lack of capital to develop natural resources, the tendency of traditional cultural and social factors to inhibit reforms, and the fragmentation of Middle and South America into a score of both large and small national states, this over-all low population density does not provide a true picture of actual conditions and prospects. Latin America may be fairly described as underpopulated in certain areas, overpopulated in others—and underdeveloped almost everywhere.

Brazil, its largest country, still has a low density, but the picture is rapidly changing. At the turn of the century, the Brazilian population was estimated at 17 million; in 1960 the figure stood at 71 million; and by 2000 A.D. it may well be over 200 million. The population-density pattern is rapidly altering in still another way; a shift is occuring from the countryside to the cities. In Colombia, for example, which has one of the highest rates of growth (3 percent) on the continent, the increase in the rural sector during the past decade has been one percent as compared to five percent in the urban sector. And the city population is expected to treble between 1945 and 1970. One reason for urban explosion in Latin America lies in the widespread *latifundium* system, where a group of large landowners discourage the modernization of agriculture while seeking to retain their vested status and power. Low productivity and grinding poverty force the surplus village inhabitants to seek a new life in the proliferating towns—only to find all too often that they have merely jumped out of the rural frying pan into the urban fire. It is distressing to realize that in Buenos Aires, Argentina, more than 600,000 persons live in substandard settlements appropriately called "*villas miserias*" (cities of misery). In Colombia, where large shack developments also surround the cities, 59 percent of the population are without access to water mains and 72 percent have no sewage system. Approximately 80 percent of the dwellings in urban areas are partially or entirely without sanitary facilities.

A feudal peasantry in the countryside and a rootless proletariat in the city slums add up to a dangerous challenge to orderly advancement in Latin America. In today's technologically-geared world, the ability of a region to raise living standards faster than births depends largely on the amount of non-human energy available. Thus North America and Europe, with roughly one-fourth of the planet's population, consume three-fourths of the energy produced. In contrast to the average North American's consumption of close to 8000 kilograms of energy in 1960, his Latin American counterpart consumed less than 1000. Because of the much higher ratio of population below 15 years of age south of the Rio Grande, energy resources have to be devoted disproportionately to "social" rather than "economic" investment, further retarding the economic growth rate.

In short, Latin America possesses in abundance all the problems stemming from a pronounced imbalance in the production-reproduction equation. Consequently, its population explosion compounds both internal tensions and the urgency to find solutions. Will the Alliance for Progress be able to provide the necessary answers in time, or will the Latin Americans in despair turn increasingly to revolutionary attempts at problem-solving—including measures such as Castroism?

From all that has been stated here, it would appear that a planetary catastrophe looms ahead unless the prevailing birth and death rates can be brought into something like their traditional equilibrium—except that, for the first time in history, equilibrium must be sought not in terms of high but of low rates. As we have seen, science has already brought about low mortality figures, and it has developed methods to provide both cheap and effective birth control on a mass basis. Therefore, the problem of controlling the present population explosion must rest ultimately not upon technological, but upon social and moral considerations. To limit deliberately human life raises ethical questions which go to the core of man's understanding of his relationship to the universe, his fellow man, and himself.

We shall return to these questions at a later stage. Meanwhile, it is relevant to emphasize here that the scope and urgency of these questions are unprecedented; and for the first time in mankind's experience the relationship between population growth, technological change, and the use of human and animal resources has been recognized as an international challenge by the member states of the United Nations.

Topics for Discussion:

1. To what extent has medical technology been responsible for the contemporary "population explosion"?
2. Do you believe there is a "ceiling" on the number of people which our planet can sustain? What do you think is the maximal figure? What is the optimal figure, i.e., population as related to economic productivity?
3. Is the "population explosion" primarily an (a) economic, (b) political, (c) social, or (d) moral problem?
4. What has been the traditional approach to population control on the part of (a) Hinduism, (b) Islam, (c) Roman Catholicism, (d) Marxism?
5. Is reduction in fertility rates an inevitable consequence of either industrialization or urbanization? Explain.
6. Discuss whether the United States Government should provide free food from its agricultural surpluses to countries whose chronically undernourished peoples make no effort to control their numbers?
7. As the available living space in the "lower latitudes" (in the technologically-backward tropics) fills up, would you favor relaxing the present immigration restrictions to permit large-scale settlement of non-Caucasian peoples in low-density areas within the United States? If not, how would you meet the charge that you are practicing racial discrimination, or *apartheid* and if mass starvation increases, a form of genocide?
8. To what extent does a large population increase the power and political prestige of a country? To what extent can it act as a source of weakness for a nation?

6

Natural Resources:

FUTURE PLENTY OR PENURY?

The "Road to Survival"

As a corollary of the preceding section, two basic questions have to be asked: (1) can a proliferating population be sustained by intelligent exploitation of the earth's natural resources; and (2) can these same resources also be conserved in sufficient quantity to ensure that we do not leave a "plundered planet" to the generations yet unborn? In every normal family, savings, life insurance, and other means are employed to provide for continuity in security and living standards from one generation to the next; failure to make such provision is considered prodigal and irresponsible. Is the planetary family now prudent or extravagant? As some ecologists have asked, are we prepared to make an inventory of our planetary resources—and depletions—and use wisely what remains?

Water: Increasingly in Short Supply

Water is indispensable to all forms of life. Though it exists as a constant amount on this planet, only a relatively small portion is available at present for human use. Much is locked in glaciers and ice caps, and the oceans which cover three-fourths of the earth's surface contain so much mineral matter they are unfit for human consumption. Land-based organisms, including mankind, exist only because of natural processes by which a very small fraction of ocean water daily changes its form and composition and moves to places where these organisms can receive it. As a result of this hydrologic cycle, water on the ocean surface is transformed by solar radiation into water vapor which is diffused upward into the atmosphere, to be condensed into drops of water as a result of the cooling of an air mass. Water becomes a usable resource, however, only from the time it strikes the land until it reënters the ocean or some other body of water, and only so long as it remains more or less pure. Some of the water stays on the surface. A large portion sinks into the soil where it is sometimes caught in subterranean reservoirs such as those located deep under the Sahara Desert. The amount of water available for human use is far from limitless. Unfortunately, it is unequally distributed both among the earth's major regions and also within the confines of each country.

Moreover, the normal movement of the hydrologic cycle can be severely impaired, thereby reducing the amount of water available to men. Destruction of the plant cover, such as by deforestation and over grazing, can lead to removal of the sponge-like texture of the complex topsoil and to the onslaught of erosion, the "cancer of the land." As the soil's capacity to absorb rain water diminishes, water tables fall. When the water cannot sink into the ground, it must run off the surface, carrying soil with it to clog up rivers and lakes. This in turn causes costly floods. Ancient societies in Mesopotamia and North Africa fell prey to the dislocation of the hydrologic cycle. Never before, however, has a bad dislocation of the hydrologic cycle involved so many hundreds of millions of people.

The demand for water in all lands is growing at an accelerating pace. This is due to the increase not only in the population of the world but also of the rates of consumption by individuals, industry, and agriculture. Sanitation requirements have risen markedly during this century; many industrial processes utilize water on an unprecedented scale; and in arid countries, especially, population pressures demand costly new irrigation networks and the construction of great reservoirs to retain more of a river's water before it is lost to the sea. The gravity of the problem is underscored by the erection of the High Dam at Aswan, Egypt; the extensive acreage which its captured waters can bring under cultivation will be required just to sustain the exploding Egyptian population at much the same low living standards existing when construction of the dam began.

Wise use of the planet's waters—perhaps our most precious single resource—requires governmental action simultaneously at all levels: municipal, state, federal, and international. The primary goal is an abundant supply of clean drinking water. In Turkey, for example, one problem that demands attention is the shortage of drinking water for the approximately 30,000 villages and small rural settlements whose seven million inhabitants must subsist on minimum quantities of muddy, impure water obtained from springs or wells by arduous manual labor and transported long distances on the shoulders of women and children. In the United

States and Canada, where very different technological and living standards exist from those in Turkey (or again in India with its hundreds of
thousands of villages and their no less impure wells and springs), a danger-
ously—and disgracefully—high proportion of the rivers have become
polluted by raw sewage and untreated industrial waste. Looking into the
future, we must also recognize the growing health risks from an increasing
reliance upon nuclear forms of energy-production, unless exceptional care
is taken in the disposing of radioactive waste in order to prevent contamination of water resources.

Although the total amount of water on the planet cannot be increased,
it is possible to find additional sources for man's use. For the immediate
future, surface and ground water comprise the two chief sources. As in
ancient days hydraulic engineers constructed canals to bring surface
water to Nineveh and Babylon, and aqueducts to supply Rome, so today a
system of conduits brings hundreds of millions of gallons daily to New
York City from streams 160 miles distant in the Adirondacks. A new
system of dams, tunnels, and aqueducts has been built in Australia to
transfer water (which would otherwise flow from the Snowy Mountains
southeastward to the ocean) to the western side of the range to help
irrigate semi-arid but potentially cultivable plains. Some diversion of
water also takes place across America's Continental Divide. In 1964, the
water level of the Great Lakes fell to a point critically low for seaway
shipping and the needs of the great urban complexes situated on both
sides of the international boundary. The longer-term implications have
raised the question—and challenge—of diverting water to the Upper Great
Lakes from rivers which at present empty into Hudson Bay.

In the vast semi-arid belt extending across North Africa, the Middle
East, and the central Eurasian land mass, ground water offers the principal additional source. Extensive geological and related studies will have
to be undertaken at both the national and international levels to locate
these underground basins in the Sahara, Gobi, and elsewhere. The discov-
ery of even comparatively small underground supplies can alter conditions significantly in desert environments. This was shown in Syria where
sufficient water has been tapped in its desert pastureland to support an
additional 1,300,000 sheep. Meanwhile, in the United States, the Soviet
Union, and Israel, massive efforts are being made to find economical
methods for desalinizing ocean water. New York City now plans to build
an atomic desalinization plant, the tenth in the world. If it produces fresh
water economically, a permanent solution may have been found to mankind's perennial, and increasing, water problems.

Since water sources do not respect boundaries, their availability often
depends less upon technological than upon political factors. In 1964,
Canada and the United States amicably concluded a treaty on the use of
Columbia River water and hydroelectric power, and in recent years India
and Pakistan agreed to share the waters of the Indus River. In sharp

contrast, Israel and its Arab neighbors have bitterly contested the use of the Jordan, and unilateral diversion by either side of that river's waters—indispensable to agriculture in that parched region—could well start a new Israeli-Arab war. The largest river in southeast Asia, the Mekong, has a rich economic potential, not only to provide electricity in huge amounts but also to irrigate hundreds of thousands of acres and thereby enormously increase the production of rice and other basic crops. The United Nations has provided considerable technical assistance to help initiate a multipurpose developmental project in the Lower Mekong Basin, and President Johnson has offered to ask Congress to join in a billion dollar American investment in this effort when it is underway. Four riparian countries—Thailand, Laos, Cambodia, and Vietnam—must also collaborate, however, if it is to come into existence. This cooperation in turn must await a solution of the dangerous political situation at present dividing the peoples of southeast Asia.

Land: Its Use and Misuse

Without soil there can be no life. The teeming billions of insects and humans who inhabit this globe ultimately depend upon a relatively few inches' thickness of this resource—itself the highly complex product of geological, climatic, and biological factors—to live. Of the 28 percent of the planet's surface comprising land, 30 percent is in forest, 19 percent is in pasture and meadow, while 10 percent is arable or in tree crops. This means that mankind is being kept alive on the produce of less than 3 percent of the earth's total surface and upon the 5 percent comprising grassland. In 1959, the amount of arable land totaled one acre per person, a figure that will drop to about a quarter of an acre by the year 2050. This means that the average acre will then have to produce about four times as much as it does now.

The use to which land is put, however, is never static. Much of the best arable land is being gradually lost, as shown by the disheartening fact that almost half of the total cultivated area in the world is subject to erosion. Farming land is being diminished—often as a result of poor planning—by urban sprawl: new residential developments, factory sites, roads and highways, airport installations, and reservoirs for water supplies. On the other hand, new farming lands are being brought into use by reclamation from the sea (as in the case of Dutch polders), by ploughing of grasslands, by irrigation of desert and semi-arid areas, and by the clearance of forests.

Much land which, in its natural state, possesses unproductive soil can be brought under cultivation by the addition of fertilizers. The sandy soils of Long Island and eastern New Jersey, for instance, are employed in profitable truck-gardening operations to meet the massive demands of New York City. The use of fertilizers differs greatly from region to region. Europe leads in intensity of use, while the lowest consumption is in Africa.

There are wide variations among countries and within regions. If even modest levels of nutrition are to be obtained by 1980, the less developed parts of the world must increase their consumption of plant nutrients by 39,500,000 metric tons per year—more than the total world consumption per year during the period 1956 to 1960.

By 2000 A.D., half of the world's population may be urban. Fortunately, from the standpoint of the population explosion, far more people can be fed off an acre than on it. This has been the case ever since the farmers of the ancient fluvial civilizations began to acquire food surpluses that could sustain city-dwellers. Today, in the United States, only 9 percent of the labor force is employed on the land, while British agriculture, the most highly mechanized in the world, permits one farm worker to feed 40 other persons. That the Western countries can produce so abundantly with such a relatively small labor force is due to advanced mechanization. Of the 11,063,000 tractors in use in world farming in 1960, 9,800,000 could be found in North America, Europe, and the Soviet Union.

In contrast, the remainder of the world has to rely not upon the machine's horsepower but upon the muscle power of the peasant, sometimes augmented by that of his draft animal. Since muscle power depends upon food calories, it has been described as "the most expensive power in the world." This fact, coupled with the other inefficient techniques employed in subsistence farming in underdeveloped regions, explains productivity levels so low that mass hunger is endemic and famine a recurrent experience. Thus, while the European farmer was able in 1960 to produce 1,903 kilograms of wheat and 4,400 kilograms of rice from a given unit of space, his counterpart in Africa succeeded in harvesting only 570 and 1,110 kilograms of each crop.

If the efficiency of the planet's farming land is to be maximized, agricultural stagnation in Asia, Africa, and Latin America must give way to massive reforms on a broad front. Soils must be improved by correct use of chemical fertilizers and the construction of large-scale irrigation and drainage projects. Such reforms must be accompanied by improved plant breeding in order to provide greater resistance to disease and pests and to increase crop yields. As a result of Japanese rice breeding, for example, annual production of that cereal rose from 7,500,000 metric tons when breeding work began to 12,500,000. Likewise, animal resources must be improved. In India and parts of Africa, religious or social customs have permitted excessive numbers of poorly bred and fed cattle to exist at the expense of the human family. Modern livestock management calls also for reduction in animal disease, improvement in breeding strains, and measures to insure that pasture land is not over grazed. An up-to-date dairy technology could provide the people of underdeveloped lands with more animal protein and a better balanced intake of vitamins and minerals. A much larger portion of the world's aquatic resources needs to be "farmed" in order to raise nutritional standards. Fresh-water and marine fisheries in

1962 produced 41,200,000 metric tons; yet some authorities maintain that this figure can be increased three-fold, arguing that fish, seaweed, and algae comprise the least exploited of the earth's food resources.

It has been estimated that one-third of the human race does not get enough of the right kind of food, while about 10 to 15 percent simply does not get enough to eat. The vicious circle of "poverty-malnutrition-disease-low productivity-poverty" has been one of the important reasons why many countries in Asia, Africa, and Latin America have not taken major strides in developing their natural resources. The gap in living standards between the "rich" and "poor" nations could one day set off regional—and even racial—conflicts of unprecedented magnitude and bitterness.

Man's Use of Forests and Minerals

Linked with agriculture in transforming the soil's fertility into raw materials for men's use is forestry. We have already noted that forests, which cover nearly one-third of the earth's surface, play an indispensable protective role in soil conservation and flood control. This role has been tragically ignored both by the farmer seeking fresh land to cultivate and by the logger exploiting timber stands for his immediate profit. About 40 percent of the world's forests are inaccessible, while another 24 percent have not yet been exploited. Much of the total forest area lies in the tropics, where wood remains a major raw material for both building and fuel. Consequently, the peoples concerned need to develop forest management in order to plan, utilize, and conserve their timber resources and integrate them into their overall national economies. Since forests comprise a renewable resource, they represent an invaluable asset to present and future generations alike.

Mineral resources, on the other hand, present a double-edged problem; they are useless unless developed, but they are the product of age-old geological processes and are consequently nonreplenishable. Without being properly utilized, they cannot enable a nation to raise its living standards and assume its rightful place in today's world. At the same time, a wise developmental program must surely accept the principle of conservation to provide for long-term as well as immediate needs. The difficulties posed for the decision-makers are compounded by the fact that the value of a given mineral resource largely depends upon the existing state of technology, a process always undergoing change. For example, the first industrial revolution was based upon steam, a form of energy produced by coal, as the prime mover. Subsequently, the invention of the internal-combustion engine called for the large-scale extraction of petroleum, so that coal has declined in relative value in our own century. Would it have been "right" for the industrialists a hundred years ago to have foregone—in the name of conservation—the maximum use of available coal resources? By so doing they would have slowed down industrial and economic growth when, as it happened, coal was to be progressively superseded by a technology depending increasingly upon oil and hydro-generated electricity. This in turn may eventually be replaced by nuclear fuels. In short, to what extent are we justified in taking little heed of tomorrow's mineral requirements because of an up-dated admonition that reads "sufficient unto the day be the technology thereof"?

There can be no simple answer. Yet we know that the accelerating requirements for raw materials will make inroads upon the earth's non-replenishable resources far beyond the demands so far experienced—and these have already been unprecedented. Nearly one-half of all the oil and gas ever consumed in the United States has been burned since 1940. Furthermore, this country has "creamed off" the richest ores of the iron de-posits of Mesabi, once considered to be virtually inexhaustible. As long ago as 1960, imports of iron ore accounted for nearly 35 percent of U.S. consumption, although they comprised less than 10 percent a decade earlier. Little domestic ore can compete on a qualitative basis with for-eign ore, unless it is first treated and its iron content is upgraded. We are fortunate that the known reserves of iron ore amount to at least 106 billion tons in the non-Communist World alone, and new fields continue to be discovered in Canada and elsewhere. Even so, we cannot afford to be complacent. It has been estimated that as population increases and in-dustrialization spreads around the globe, the quantity of steel in use may rise in the foreseeable future to 70 billion tons, while the demand for copper, lead, and zinc could total approximately one billion tons. The world's demand for minerals and metals more than doubled between 1930 and 1960—*and it is expected to double again, this time by 1970.*

Energy Resources

The production of energy is essential to all economic activity. Paleolith-ic man had to rely upon his own muscle power; his Mesolithic successor proceeded to domesticate the dog in order to pull his sled; while his Neolithic descendants succeeded in domesticating a wide variety of other animals to provide food and haulage alike. Human and animal muscle power was progressively augmented—and at length largely superseded—by other prime movers: wind, water, steam, electricity, and now nuclear power. However, the development of nonbiological forms of energy-production has been confined almost exclusively to the West.

It has been estimated that between 1 A.D. and 1850, the total input to the world energy system amounted to between 6 Q and 9 Q ("Q" being defined as equivalent to 38 billion tons of bituminous coal). In marked contrast, the rate of growth in the *per capita* demand for energy is such that we will need total inputs of 10 Q by 2000 A.D. and some 70 Q by 2050 A.D. Apart from muscle power, energy is derived from two sources, which one authority has differentiated as "income" and "capital." The former comprises fuel wood, water and wind power, solar heat collectors, tides, and natural steam. Some of these sources, such as tides and natural steam, are limited to special sites that permit either the release through the earth's crust of steam or hot water from below the surface, or the harnessing of tidal fluctuations capable of generating electricity economically. The latter type of power-production has been suggested for Passamoquoddy Bay between the state of Maine and New Brunswick, Canada.

Considerable experimentation is taking place with solar energy for heating water, cooking, distilling salt water, and producing limited amounts of power. This form of energy production can be exploited best in regions exposed to almost continuous sunshine, and especially those which are arid or semi-arid, possess little fossil fuel reserves, and lack hydraulic resources. But by and large, it is not expected that the "income" group will provide for more than 15 percent of the total energy demand for the next century.

The energy-producers comprising the "capital" group are fossil, non-replenishable fuels such as coal, oil gas, oil shale, and tar sands, as well as uranium and thorium. We have already noted our heavy reliance thus far upon coal and petroleum. Were we to remain dependent upon these sources alone, the long-term energy prospects of this planet could well give rise to anxiety. However, nuclear sources exist in abundance; some 25 million tons of uranium and one million tons of thorium are economically recoverable. The reserves of "low cost" nuclear fuels could produce 20 times as much energy as those of "low cost" coal-oil-gas (575 Q compared with 27 Q). If great expansion of electrification should occur, nuclear fuels could support most of the maximum plausible energy systems of the United States and the Free World for several centuries. Since the underdeveloped regions do not possess sufficiently large reserves of "conventional" fossil fuels to sustain industrialized economies for any significant length of time, the recent technological exploitation of nuclear fuels should be hailed as perhaps the greatest single breakthrough to realizing on a planetary scale the "revolution of rising expectations." As one observer has noted:

We must recognize that we are approaching a time when, barring a world catastrophe, men the world over will have to gain their livelihood from the lowest common denominators of the earth's crust—air, sea-water, ordinary rock, and sunlight. Air will provide us, on an expanding scale, with nitrogen for agriculture. From sea-water we will obtain fresh water, some metals, and some salts. Ordinary rock will provide us with the majority of metals, phosphorus and carbon, and the greater part of our energy. Sunlight will continue to provide energy for agriculture, and will provide as well some space heating, together with power for certain specialized purposes.[1]

On this basis, technology holds out the promise of a bright planetary future, if its accomplishments can restore the growing imbalance between a sky-rocketing population and an equally accelerating diminution of our present nonreplenishable natural resources. Meanwhile, we have scarcely the right to squander an inheritance that belongs to the future generations no less than to our own.

Topics for Discussion:

1. Why has erosion been described as the "cancer of the land"? What are the major causes of soil-erosion, and how can it be prevented?
2. Would you favor development of an international river valley authority on the (a) Jordan; (b) Mekong? To what extent can such development programs reduce political tensions and prevent fighting?
3. Discuss the long-term implications resulting from an economically successful process of large-scale desalinization.
4. It has been said that "For the first time in the history of the world, every human being is now subjected to contact with dangerous chemicals, from the moment of conception until death. In the less than two decades of their use, the synthetic pesticides have been so thoroughly distributed throughout the animate and inanimate world that they occur virtually everywhere."[2] Do you feel that present-day use of massive amounts of chemicals to control pests and raise food production may be poisoning the environment and upsetting the "balance of nature," with possibly fatal long-term results? How would you deal with the problem?
5. Discuss the possibilities of a north-south "Cold War" resulting from the widening gaps in economic growth rates between the technologically advanced and the underdeveloped countries. Can this situation be remedied and, if so, how would you set about doing it?
6. Has our generation the right to exploit the natural resources of the world to the fullest possible extent, or has it the moral obligation to regard its mission as holding them "in trust" for generations yet to be born? What arguments could be mustered for both points of view?
7. Discuss the problems that can arise in a given region following the exhaustion of its principal nonreplenishable resources.
8. Do you believe that science and technology can keep abreast of man's capacity to "plunder our planet" of nonreplenishable minerals and fuels? Do we, in effect, live in an "age of faith" no less far-reaching in its implications than that of our medieval ancestors?
9. The world's population is rising, but its natural resources are falling— and both are happening at an accelerating pace. What are the implications of this phenomenon for the decades ahead?

7

Technology's Possibilities and Problems

The Acceleration of Knowledge

Traditionally, mankind has suffered from a scarcity of knowledge and of adequate means for its dissemination. This situation still plagues the underdeveloped countries, but in economically advanced societies it has been replaced by the opposite problem; a plethora of information requiring digestion. This makes it increasingly difficult for specialists to keep abreast of developments in their own fields of knowledge. Meanwhile, the decision-makers of our society are faced with having to relate this mounting mass of information to the ever-changing needs of the most complex political, economic, and social structure in history. The speed at which knowledge is accelerating can be better realized from the following examples: the number of book titles in the world and the sizes of most of the great libraries double in approximately twenty years; while the number of scientific papers recorded by *Physics Abstracts* since it came into existence in 1900 has steadily doubled at a rate even faster than once every fifteen years. Moreover, because the single greatest outpouring of new knowledge is taking place on the frontiers of science, both theoretical and applied, it is the possibilities—and problems—of technology which will weigh most heavily upon the decision to be taken by our leaders in the decades ahead.

The Revolution in Space

Men have long sought to conquer space, yet they have achieved their goal only in this century. Indeed, the great physicist Lord Kelvin declared in 1896, only seven years before controllable manned power was attained, "I have not the smallest molecule of faith in aerial navigation other than the ballooning." As late as 1910, the British Secretary of State for War announced, "We do not consider that airplanes will be of any possible use for war purposes." He was proved wrong within half a decade by World War I; the interwar years saw the advent of commercial aviation on a continental and transoceanic scale; and World War II gave birth to military rockets.

Today, we appear to have within our reach worldwide communication, weather observation and prediction, and ship navigation systems—all because of satellites. In addition, intercontinental ballistic missiles with nuclear payloads can be trained on targets a third of the distance around the globe which, in turn, has been circled many times by Soviet cosmonauts and American astronauts. Other space vehicles have escaped the earth's gravitational pull to take pictures of both sides of the Moon, register the temperature of Venus' atmosphere, and sweep on to become permanent satellites of the Sun itself. Thus far, manned vehicles have conquered inner space, leaving to unmanned vehicles the initial intrusions into outer space with its unique and hazardous environmental problems. Yet our technology appears capable of surmounting these problems and of justifying expectations that, before the end of the same century that was ushered in with a twelve-second flight by the Wright brothers, earthlings will be speeding toward the distant planets of our solar system.

Nevertheless, we should not allow these spectacular successes to blind us to the massive problems created by the space revolution. From 1955 to 1961, the federal government appropriated some $4½ billion for various space programs; in 1962 these appropriations increased by an additional $3 billion. The President's budget for the fiscal year 1966 called for an outlay of $5 billion, and it seems certain that costs will continue to soar as more ambitious programs are implemented. Officials of the National Aeronautics and Space Administration are reported as having estimated the cost of a three-man mission to the moon at from $20 billion to $40 billion. In addition, the Defense Department (which was allocated $49 billion out of the total national budget of $99.7 billion for the fiscal year 1966) can be expected to spend additional billions on military space programs during the coming decade. Despite criticisms by some scientists that a balanced space-research program should take precedence over moonshots, and that much of the money being allocated could be better employed in medical research, in improving our educational system, and in urban renewal, the American government and public alike consider this country to be locked in a prestige race with the Soviet Union to reach the moon first. Hundreds of thousands of persons are now directly employed in the missile industry, and space programs will continue to demand highly specialized skills. These programs in turn will accelerate technological change and economic growth by, among other things, creating more efficient means of communication through satellites, smaller nuclear motors, and the development of new plastics and other synthetics. The challenges raised by complex space missions demand new responses which must affect our entire industrial and economic structure.

But man's take-off from the earth also raises vast political questions on whose answers our collective fate may depend. Who "owns" this space? In trying to answer the central question of the extent to which a nation's sovereignty extends vertically, some scholars have invoked the old Roman maxim from private law: *Cujus est solum, ejus est usque ad coelum* (Who owns the land owns it up to the sky). Unfortunately, perhaps, the sky is not a fixed boundary, nor does the atmosphere lend itself to clear-cut gradations. At first it was argued that the atmosphere could be divided into zones, but these were based on standards which technological advances rendered successively obsolete. International jurists have not yet been able to agree on a boundary line between "inner" space—over which the subjacent state must be able to exercise some control—and "outer" space which, like the high seas, should logically be considered international and not susceptible to appropriation by any nation.

Here we are dealing with a subject that is anything but academic and remote in its implications; to permit the arms race to merge with the space race could result in the orbiting of outer space platforms capable of raining thermonuclear destruction upon defenseless countries and subjecting entire continents to the blackmail of surrender-or-death. In 1963, the United Nations called on all nations to refrain from placing weapons of mass destruction in orbit, and it also declared that outer space and celestial bodies must be utilized for the benefit of all mankind. These are surely moves in the right direction as plans proceed to land earthlings on the Moon before the end of this decade, while the construction of space platforms will one day set the stage for launching larger vehicles for interplanetary probes.

The "Balance of Terror"

Technology begot the space race; it has also revolutionized the arms race. It is common knowledge that the postwar years have unleashed the most expensive and lethal buildup of armaments in history. World War II stimulated the production of weapons of unparalleled destructive power, including innovations in chemical and biological warfare which, if not employed at that time, are to be found today in the arsenals of all major countries. In 1945, Hiroshima and Nagasaki were pulverized by the first primitive nuclear bombs. Japan's immediate surrender underscored the fact that, with its atomic monopoly, the United States could have imposed its will upon any other nation as well. This monopoly ended in September 1949 with the detonation of the first Soviet nuclear device. Since then scientists have produced the hydrogen bomb together with a highly sophisticated intercontinental ballistics delivery system, while the nuclear club has steadily increased to include the United Kingdom, France, and Communist China. In 1965, the Indonesian government declared that it, too, would become a nuclear power before the year was out. Although this boast still has not been fulfilled, the stark fact remains that, in a world still subject to the rule of force, an accelerating proliferation of nuclear powers must be expected. Each new addition geometrically complicates effective international inspection and control of atomic weapons.

In the absence of such control, the nuclear powers have been engaging in Operation "Overkill," that is, in producing bombs far in excess of the numbers theoretically required to exterminate each other's population. As a consequence, their decision-makers can initiate a holocaust that could destroy hundreds of millions of people in a few hours. Because Washington and Moscow can ensure retaliation of this magnitude, a rough-and-ready power balance has been attained—a "balance of terror." To remain effective, this requires a continuing equilibrium in the overall striking effectiveness of the protagonists but, unfortunately, technological invention accelerates the drive to obsolescence even as it escalates the striking potential to a new order of magnitude. Since each protagonist must assume that its rival is about to score a "break-through" to a new destructive capability, it in turn must do its utmost to help upset the very balance upon which the present deterrence alone rests.

It would seem sensible to reverse the direction of progressive escalation by disarming. However, to "de-escalate" would require the same rigorous maintenance of balance between the nuclear giants, since a unilateral act of reduction by one side could upset the balance in favor of the other camp. So far, the great powers have not been able to find any acceptable formula either for disarmament or even for international arms inspection.

The problem of arms reduction, not to mention general disarmament, is compounded by the fact that military programs are massively involved in national economies. In a dozen states in the United States for example, defense payrolls account for from 10 to 30 percent of all employment in manufacturing. Obviously, any genuine shift from such expenditures would pose profound problems of dislocation. Yet it has become increasingly apparent that neither Washington nor Moscow can continue to spend upwards of half its national budget on defense and still meet its numerous other commitments, both domestic and foreign. The two nuclear giants had evinced willingness to begin to apply brakes to the costliest arms race in history when, in 1963, they signed the Moscow Treaty partially banning nuclear weapons tests—a step designed to reduce both atmospheric contamination and political tensions.

The nuclear confrontation has produced a significant factor in the war —peace equation. This is the initiative undertaken by the United Nations to mobilize and direct small peacekeeping forces—contributed by "middle powers" such as Canada and the Scandinavian countries—to prevent local "brushfires" from escalating into nuclear wars. By use of such mobile forces, which can be airlifted quickly to trouble spots anywhere on the earth's surface, the United Nations has interposed its "blue helmets" between warring armies—as in Palestine, Gaza, and Cyprus—and thereby has also prevented the existing power vacuum from being filled by the nuclear powers in direct confrontation. The overall political effectiveness of the world organization depends upon the willingness of the major members to provide the funds to enable it to continue in its peacekeeping role.

The Cold War: East-West or North-South?

The years since World War II have been marked, as we have noted in Chapter 1, by an ideological struggle between the Western and Communist camps; this Cold War has created competing military alliances and threatened at times to break into uncontrollable conflict. Yet the original solidarity characterizing these alliances has given way in the 1960's to considerable disarray with the divergence of policies within each camp and insistence upon greater national freedom of action. In the Free World, for example, the reëstablishment of Western Europe as a vigorous economic and political region has expressed itself not only in the creation of a Common Market linking France, West Germany, Italy, Belgium, The Netherlands, and Luxembourg, but also has encouraged President de Gaulle to seek to create a European "third force" under French leadership and thereby challenge the primacy of the United States in the Western alliance. Despite such divisive tendencies, it appears in 1966 that the Free World is physically strong and alert, and can face the future with justifiable confidence.

Meanwhile, the original monolithic unity imposed by Moscow upon the Communist Bloc has to some extent come apart. Since the death of Stalin and his repressive policies, the Russian people have called increasingly for the consumption of more goods at home and of more ideas from abroad. The east European satellites in turn have insisted upon greater autonomy and the reëstablishment of traditional cultural and economic ties with the West; these pressures have been especially marked in Hungary, Poland, and Rumania. Moreover, Moscow's leadership in the Communist World has been challenged by Peking, which has carried this struggle into South Asia, Africa, and even Latin America. The downfall of Khrushchev from power in 1964 forestalled what had been shaping up as a fierce showdown between Moscow and Peking, which could well have been followed by an open split among the Communist governments and a permanent polarization of rival forces around the two giants. However, as the latter months of 1965 attested, Peking's rulers accuse Khrushchev's successors of being no less "revisionist" and of conspiring with the United States to retain a virtual atomic monopoly at the expense of China and the Afro-Asian nations. The Communist World has indisputably lost its monolithic façade —and with it the myth of "historical inevitability" so assiduously fostered by Communists in the past.

That the east-west Cold War—in which two power groupings were held together by competing ideologies—has lessened in its intensity may be due to various reasons; among them is the belated recognition on both sides that, since neither dare forcibly destroy the other because of the nuclear stalemate, they must learn to coexist. Still another reason is the impact of technology upon post-war economic development. Western economies have enjoyed boom conditions as a result of increasing productivity, which in turn has benefited not only from technological advances but also from more effective teamwork by government, business, and labor. Consequently, our present "affluent society" has gone far to alter the traditional class-versus-mass economic attitudes and voting patterns— as was attested in the 1964 presidential elections which saw both big business and labor unions support the same candidate against an opponent who took a more radical stand, this time on the right.

Meanwhile, what has been described as today's "decline of ideology" seems to have affected Soviet society to the point where Marxist-Leninist-Stalinist theories are being increasingly subjected to the pressures of new social attitudes. The younger—and more sophisticated—Russians display little of the militancy that marked a revolution which took place before their birth; they insist upon greater freedom of thought and expression for their poets and artists. Their rebellion against the canons of "Soviet realism"—by which the party insisted upon calendar-type art glorifying Socialist Man while forbidding nonrepresentational painting, Freudian psychology, or even rock-and-roll because they exemplified Western "decadence"—continues to give Soviet authorities cause for alarm. The reason is not hard to find. To capitulate to this rebellion means having to recognize that ultimately the "human condition" is more significant in men's lives than arid ideology, and that the previous simplistic dogma which portrayed Communism as all good and Western liberalism as all bad is neither true nor, worse still from the standpoint of home consumption, any longer credible.

If the affluent society is undermining the dynamics of an east-west ideological confrontation, this situation has not removed the spectre of the Cold War. On the contrary, a new pattern of tensions is fast taking shape between the technologically advanced, prosperous nations of the north temperate zone and the underdeveloped, densely populated regions of the tropics. According to the United Nations Secretary-General, more people are suffering from want than ever before. In 1964 the British Foreign Secretary warned that unless drastic steps were taken to close the widening gap in living standards between the rich and poor nations, imperialism would simply have been replaced by pauperism—carrying with it "a bitterness accentuated perhaps by racial hatred." This bitterness is born of a feeling of desperation among non-Western people that their hard-won political independence may prove an empty victory unless technology can be employed to enable goods to be produced faster than population, and is presently being exploited by Communist China in its bid for leadership. Unless checked, a north-south Cold War—or worse—looms ahead.

In the long run, technology promises to be able to raise living standards on every continent, but the peril lies in coping with the massive immediate problems, which are at once political, economic, and psychological. Thus, technical and financial assistance must come from the richer "donor" nations which are prompted to help for a variety of reasons. Apart from the humanitarian motive, one reason is the desire to win friends and influence government leaders in the poorer "recipient" countries; another is to meet the ideological competition of other donors. Such motives are not lost upon the recipient governments which, in turn, often display no less opportunism and cynicism in playing off one potential donor against another—thereby subjecting both Washington and Moscow to a fairly obvious form of blackmail. When so much aid is predicated upon political objectives, imbalance in economic programming can occur, so that the recipient countries may fail to achieve maximum industrial growth.

Again, the decision-makers of the underdeveloped nations are faced with a vast array of difficult problems. They must decide, for instance, how to update agricultural methods and increase agricultural production when ancient methods are firmly set in the mind of the populace. Given the fact that resources are in most instances limited, which industries should be developed? Should the aim of investment be an immediate high return of capital or more balanced growth and a slower return?

There can be little doubt that the present pattern of foreign aid provides frustrations and irritations alike for the donor nations, which believe that their generosity is all too often exploited and then villified, and for the recipients, which feel in turn that they are regarded as charity cases or else as pawns in some international chess game manipulated by the great powers. Perhaps some of these problems could be remedied if more of the present bilateral aid were directed into multilateral channels, and if the burdens of foreign assistance were equitably distributed among all the economically advanced nations. But meanwhile, there are good reasons—both hard-headed as well as soft-hearted—to justify continuing foreign aid until technology and economic progress enable the developing countries to stand on their own feet.

Triumph of the Technological Order

This century has been marked by two dynamic forces which, taken together, create a paradoxical situation. The first is nationalism by which the peoples of Asia and Africa have thrown off colonial tutelage and are insisting upon recognition of their indigenous culture patterns and value systems—an insistence accompanied by rejection of many Western political standards and institutions. At the same time, on the economic level, Africans and Asians demand massive technical and developmental aid which can only accelerate the very processes that are destroying traditional rural, village-centered forms of social organization and values, and are forcing increasing numbers to the mushrooming cities where industrialism, secularism, and urban wants are dominant. In short, the dynamics of the technological order are progressively eroding the indigenous Asian and African culture patterns at the very time when those continents have acquired political emancipation from the West, and are substituting for these patterns what begins to approximate the Western "way of life."

Actually, this break-up of traditional societal patterns in Asia and Africa, even though spectacular because of the speed and timing involved, is but a continuation of a similar process that was set in motion earlier in the West. From early modern times, Western society has been undergoing rapid alterations: of population from the countryside to the town, of family organization and size, and of ethical and moral behavior patterns based upon traditional religious beliefs. The non-Western world is discovering what the Western World has already had to recognize, namely, that Western society is inextricably geared to the technological order. In the final analysis, it is this technology, which has harnessed the atom's Promethean fire, that distinguishes "Civilization Present" from "Civilization Past." We must expect it to become fully planetary in dimensions and dynamics alike before the end of this century.

Automation: Friend or Foe?

"The major domestic challenge of the Sixties," President Kennedy declared, was to "maintain full employment at a time when automation is replacing men." He pointed out that over a ten-year period, some 25,000 new jobs would have to be found every week "to take care of those displaced by machines and those who are coming into the labor market."[1] Though a comparatively new word, "automation" is hardly a new phenomenon; after all, the steam engine mechanized industrial production, a stage carried much further in turn by the electric motor. The term is applied now to those processes of mechanization that are controlled by electronic devices which can also compute in advance the rate at which materials are assembled and production determined.

Automation has certain obvious advantages. It allows us to relegate burdensome and repetitious manual tasks to machines which in turn can perform them with a speed and precision that human hands can never equal. What is more, automation is part of a sophisticated technology that has stepped up production in spectacular fashion; industrial output in the

United States has been doubling every 25 to 30 years while the population has been doubling every 45 to 50 years. This is the chief reason for our rising living standards.

Meanwhile, automated production has various organizational and psychological impacts upon workers, though studies in this area are far from complete. For example, although the new processes involve less physical effort—and much less handling of heavy materials—there is often much greater emotional strain because a small failure in the system may swiftly mushroom to serious proportions unless the worker is alert and takes precise remedial action. Since there are fewer workers in "push-button" factories, they are stationed farther apart. Consequently, a sense of isolation may develop; it may be harder to establish friendly working relations; and there is no longer the traditional need to form work groups with their strong sense of team effort and human interdependence.

Work in more advanced technological plants is generally rewarded with higher pay and carries with it increased prestige for the workers involved, for they are recognized as possessing special technical skills. On the other hand, the older incentive systems no longer apply; the inducement to work harder or to do "time-and-a-half" has been replaced by self-regulating mechanisms which control the rate of production that has already been "programmed" by the computer. Moreover, due to the larger capital investments relative to labor costs in the advanced machines, the scheduling of work on a 24-hour basis has become more prevalent. As a result of having to subordinate the worker's timetable to that of the production line, such around-the-clock operations require numerous workers and their families to make sizable physical and social adjustments.

Perhaps what is most disturbing psychologically and socially about the technological changes we are now confronted with is what we sense to be the extended nature of these changes and a seemingly unending and accelerating rate of change. We suspect that change is both functional and dysfunctional for the individual and for the society. What the optimum rate for each of these is we do not know.[2]

We are confronted now with an unprecedented situation: increasing economic returns with decreasing man-hours of work. How will this affect the question of unemployment? Regretably, we are given conflicting answers, based upon incomplete evidence. Labor leaders and politicians alike are worried about the possible implications. Perhaps their fears are exaggerated. The automobile destroyed the blacksmith's trade, but it transformed him into a garage mechanic or service station attendant. Automation may simply alter the present employment pattern rather than reduce the number of jobs. But previous experience cannot accurately assess the new element involved, which stems from what the philosopher Alfred North Whitehead described as the greatest invention in modern times: "the invention of the method of invention." Today, we can not only virtually automate entire industries but also "program" machines to make still other machines. None of these machines however will have what the workers whom they replace possessed: the purchasing power to buy the goods they produce.

To what extent, then, is the human factor becoming expendable? That question brings us to our final area of inquiry.

Topics for Discussion:

1. Traditionally, national sovereignty has been demarcated on the basis of two-dimensional, or "flat," space. If it cannot be demarcated on the third, or "vertical" dimension, what are the implications for the national-state system as we have known it to the present time?

2. As a corollary of the above question, how can one define "aggression" when alien intrusion occurs in airspace? Are American astronauts and Soviet cosmonauts guilty of "aggression" when they orbit the earth on flight paths that cross over numerous countries?

3. Do you believe that the billions now allocated by the United States to the "moon shot" represent money well spent? What are the implications for (a) the economy; (b) technological research; (c) America's present medical and educational needs? Would you prefer to see the Americans and Russians cooperate, or compete, in space exploration?

4. Was the United States justified in dropping atomic bombs on Hiroshima and Nagasaki in 1945? Many Africans and Asians have charged that America would not have employed the same measures against German cities (had the bombs then been available) because their populations were "Western" and "white." Do you believe there is any truth in this charge?

5. Under what circumstances, if any, would you advocate the employment of atomic weapons, chemical or germ warfare by the U.S.?

6. Do you think general disarmament is feasible? Which is the greater risk in today's world: unilateral reduction of armaments or continuation of the most massive, and lethal, arms race in history?

7. The Russians appear to be losing much of their revolutionary zeal and militancy; it is also true that their living standards have been rising. Can we draw the generalization that revolution and affluence are basically incompatible? To what extent does this generalization apply (in reverse form) to the Afro-Asian states and the possibility of a north-south Cold War?

8. If you were the chief decision-maker of a newly established, under-developed country, what would be your order of priorities in the (a) political, (b) economic, and (c) educational spheres?

9. Discuss the implications of automation from the standpoints of (a) increased productivity; (b) employment; (c) the status and "worth" of the individual worker.

8

The Individual in Mass Society

Contemporary Man: Autonomous or Automaton?

"The characteristic of the hour is that the commonplace mind, knowing itself to be commonplace, has the assurance to proclaim the rights of the commonplace and to impose them wherever it will. . . . The mass crushes beneath it everything that is different, everything that is excellent, individual, qualified, and select."[1] Is this generalization just? Ours has been termed the century of the common man, of mass thought, of mass tastes, and of political mass reactions. The historian will point out that societies have always comprised a great majority content with mass opinions and tastes and, in sharp distinction, a small creative minority with its own standards and aspirations. But the past was marked by scarcities—of material goods, of educational opportunity, and of effective communication—so that a society's tastes and policies were dictated by the affluent minority. On the other hand, in today's technological order, with its giant production lines, the same "economies of scale" which can produce a cheaper product for a national consumer market will in turn emphasize those social standards and political attitudes that only strengthen mass conformity.

In our age of agglomeration—of big business, big labor, and big government—what happens to the individual? Is he in danger of becoming "impersonalized" and even "dehumanized"—of being lost in the "faceless crowd" so that he is reduced to a social security number? Is this not an apt analogy, since in return for acquiring the security and "fringe benefits" which only an affluent society can provide, he is computerized to a numerical digit, and is treated as a mass-man? Perhaps the ultimate question confronting society in this century remains the same as for all preceding ages: what is the status to be ascribed to man as an individual? Is he to be regarded as inherently free and autonomous, in short, as the ultimate subject in a society that calls itself democratic, or is he to be manipulated as an automaton by the "hidden persuaders" and the "specialists in the hard and soft sell"?

The Pressures to Conform

We hear much these days about the widening gap in outlook and communication between the traditional humanistic culture and the accelerating technological sector. All too often, technology is damned because it has created numerous problems with which we have to cope: urban sprawl, smog, or the sonic booms which will undoubtedly increase in number, and nervous intensity, as commercial aviation acquires speeds faster than sound. But since most, if not all, of such problems can probably be overcome by further technological gains, they do not really advance our search for answers to the central issue posed above: what is our technological order doing to the status and dignity of man as an individual? At least one scholar contends that there is an inherent conflict involved which may defy solution. Thus, it is argued that since the technological order is concerned with the world of material things, its interest in man takes the form of converting him in turn into a material object. Hence, because of its method, which is quantitative and reduces all phenomena, including mankind, to that which can be measured, the technological order is incapable of understanding—far less of safeguarding—the humanistic order that is concerned with human excellence, a concept at once qualitative and not ultimately measurable.

Technological advancement has led to the growth of power on such a scale that now, for the first time in history, it can annihilate all planetary life. To utilize strength of such magnitude has called into being absolute powers of decision-making. It is argued that power eliminates, in proportion to its growth, the boundary between good and evil, between the just and the unjust, a phenomenon common to totalitarian societies. Thus the growth of technology which fosters absolutism prevents the appearance of values and our search for the ethical and spiritual. Finally, it is contended that the technological order can never engender freedom. True, it liberates man from age-old scourges such as plague and famine, but it replaces them with newer and more sophisticated constraints. Because technology is an ensemble of rational and efficient practices, of complex programs and mechanisms, it calls for order and a set process into which freedom and unorthodoxy cannot penetrate. All that these last could possibly introduce is discord and disorder. As technology plays a larger role in society, human autonomy and initiative diminish.

These pronouncements may strike us as unduly pessimistic, but we cannot dismiss them out of hand. This century has been marked by the rise of totalitarian regimes which, whether on the extreme right or left, maximized their control of the technological order in an effort to crush individual freedom and impose social conformity. In democratic societies, although one must remain vigilant to ensure that centralized authority does not infringe upon civil liberties—or engage in "news management"— the pressures to which the individual is daily subjected are much less political than social. The perils conjured up by Western novelists are not those of the police state and concentration camp but rather of English novelist Aldous Huxley's *Brave New World;* they are not of brainwashing in a North Korean prisoner-of-war camp but of "subliminal advertising" (advertising that makes an impression on the subconscious) over a national television network. Even so, let us at least recognize the presence of these constant pressures to make people conform, as individuals, to social attitudes and behavior patterns not of their own devising—and often contrary to their own preferences.

Ralph Waldo Emerson, the nineteenth-century American essayist and poet, spoke for a past generation of Americans, reared in a philosophy of staunch individualism, when he declared that "Whoso would be a man must be a nonconformist." Today's emphasis in the United States is instead upon "group thinking" and the "well-adjusted" because, whether he is a college undergraduate or an aspiring business executive, the younger American quickly learns that today's social and financial rewards go less to the nonconformist than to him who plays it "cool" and "safe," who keeps unorthodox opinions to himself, and who dares not risk offending whether by lack of diplomacy or deodorant. The search for security with its attending fringe benefits may not appear to be in the same revolutionary tradition as the events of 1776, but it finds a full quota of advocates who seek jobs as bureaucrats in an era of "creeping socialism" or, alternatively, as "organization men" in giant corporations comprising what has been called "galloping capitalism."

One observer of the contemporary American scene describes the dominant middle-class type as "other-directed," that is, the type of person who derives his aspirations and goals from his class, with little or no thought about the kind of life or environment to which he is adjusting himself. This in itself is not a new phenomenon, since throughout history most persons have conformed uncritically to traditional patterns. But whereas in the past the "others" directing group attitudes were public leaders and educators who, like Emerson, preached the virtues of American individualism and even nonconformity, today's opinion-moulders are in many cases the "silent persuaders" who hold no public or educational office and need assume no public responsibility for their actions. They include the advertising-agency men who have carried the arts of psychological assault to new levels of sophistication, and sophistry. In order to sell their commercial products they foster the values of conformity, suggesting that one should buy something because everybody is doing so. They further their cause by exploiting the common fears of being unpopular or different. In so far as they urge Americans to be different, it is by snob appeal to the status-seekers; thereby, they exploit a vulgar illusion of individuality. They have sold the idea that the main end of freedom is to indulge oneself, or in more technical terms, to be a consumer. Most people are quite willing to concentrate upon this function to their last days on earth (in an expensive casket). Unfortunately, by being faithful consumers they are unlikely to have the time or inclination to cultivate individuality.[2]

An Age of Anxiety—and Tranquilizers

Despite unprecedented social affluence and security, many people suffer from anxiety and a sense of alienation. The collective situation calls to mind one of the "morals" in James Thurber's *Fables for Our Time:* "The world is so full of a number of things, I am sure we should all be as happy as kings—and you know how happy kings are." One modern philosopher has pointed out that man engages concurrently in three conflicts: with his physical environment, with his fellow man, and with himself. The affluence that exists in some parts of the world derives principally from the spectacular gains that have attended man's use of technology to "conquer" nature; but, as we have seen previously, this very success has helped to create new problems, such as the population explosion and the impact of automation upon employment.

Man's failure to resolve conflict with his fellow man has resulted in the most costly arms race in history and the advent of the balance of nuclear terror—so that the frustrations of statesmen only compound the deep-seated anxieties of the individual citizen. Lastly, because these conflicts occur as the result of an agglomeration of impersonal forces over which the individual seems unable to exercise any control but which he feels control him, his present physical comforts do little to allay his fears and frustrations or the nagging guilt complex that compares his affluence with the poverty and hunger of the majority of mankind.

Paradoxically, the United States possesses the world's highest standard of living and perhaps the highest proportion of neurotics, while those countries in Europe which boast the most prosperous economies on that continent also have the dubious distinction of sharing the highest incidence of alcoholism and suicide. Are affluence and alcohol, success and suicide, linked only by alliteration? Or do they point unmistakably to the "human condition" in which no individual can "contract out" of the privations and pains of his fellow man, because we all have to share the same planet?

Whatever the reason, the paradox of physical security mated to psychological insecurity remains to haunt Americans, both as a society and as individuals. Because of this inner conflict, they turn to technology to find a way to ease their tension. The solution offered is tranquilizers, though these drugs have to share popularity with "pep pills" which have an opposite purpose. It is an eloquent, if disturbing, commentary upon contemporary society when sizable numbers of its citizens have to depend upon artificial means to energize and/or tranquilize them, and it is still more distressing to read of an increase in the use of barbiturates as well as the more traditional narcotic drugs. Yet it is part of a larger pattern in which medical triumphs close down sanatoria once given over to tuberculosis and other former mass-killers while, at the same time, new complexes have to be rushed to completion to cope with the many mental and nervous diseases.

It is possible, of course, that Americans are too anxious about their anxieties, even as their educational psychologists in the recent past have all too often prescribed intellectual pablum instead of roughage in a well-meaning effort to prevent the classroom diet from upsetting junior's delicately-adjusted equilibrium, of bruising his psyche. Has the United States become a land of people so medicated and shielded from physical pain that they must compulsively seek to be anaesthetized against anxiety itself, instead of recognizing its significance? No creative age in history has been devoid of tensions and dangers; indeed, these may be essential to provide the adrenalin that stimulates the Magellans—and American astronauts—to seek out new worlds. Surely, too, they are no less required to provide the moral courage to right old wrongs, however "respectable," and to confront an individual with the test of his own worth.

The Challenge to Traditional Values

Many contemporary dilemmas stem from a pervasive sense of alienation. Where commercial pressures insist upon "togetherness," a euphemism for conformity, the individual can all too easily feel, or be made to feel, that "he does not belong" within the community to which he seeks to "relate." His alienation may be due to group prejudices based on race, religion, or economic status. On the other hand, it may be a reflection of an abdication on the part of the elites—religious, political, and educational—from their traditional responsibility to provide guidelines to enable society as a whole to remain integrated and to exist in a purposeful fashion. The intellectual's task is to apply the processes of reason to both physical and social phenomena. However, in an age that has seized upon Freud's emphasis on the irrational in human behavior, the intellectual is all too often paralyzed by a lack of belief in the importance—and continuing need—of his own traditional role. Yet it is surely no less true today than in a technologically primitive time, that "Where there is no vision, the people perish."

Unfortunately, the traditional values and norms of behavior that motivated and directed pre-industrial societies are not necessarily relevant to our own day. Evidence abounds that morals are far from absolute. To take one example, it is significant that slavery was held to be moral—and even sanctioned by scripture—during those millennia when motive power had to be provided primarily by human muscles. It was the advent of the steam engine that finally rendered slavery both redundant and immoral.

We began our enquiry by pointing out that the major religions have traditionally encouraged high fertility rates. This attitude was logical because of the persistence of almost equally high death rates until the past century. Since technology has spectacularly reduced the latter, has it not also rendered uncontrolled motherhood redundant—and even immoral? Put in these terms, the question may appear to be a gross distortion of a highly complex social and ethical issue. Nevertheless, the magnitude of the problems produced by the population explosion—in terms of the utilization of limited space and resources, as well as the difficulties involved in raising living standards in underdeveloped regions—can, unless checked, doom billions to hopeless poverty and endless warfare to obtain land. Ultimately the problem is moral and, as such, poses a challenge not only to collective societal action but equally to the individual's choice of conduct. By employing birth-control techniques, he can limit reproduction but, by so doing, he also decides whether other human beings shall come into existence. If to take human life can be murder, what shall we deem the act that denies life in the first place? Who or what, furthermore, shall decide how much life is "good" for the planet, and have we succeeded in resolving the important question of the inherent worth, or sanctity, of the individual?

In raising these questions, we do not mean to imply that there are simple—or even satisfactory—answers; we are emphasizing rather that the present generation is faced with moral issues of the first magnitude for which there is often no historical precedent. For example, American society has traditionally taught that it is good, indeed essential, to work hard, to be thrifty and save, to avoid self-indulgence and idleness; in short, they have been instructed to abide by Benjamin Franklin's advice and what is sometimes called the "Puritan ethic". To work hard in this decade may deprive another American of his job, whereas "featherbedding" can provide two pay packets instead of just one. To be thrifty and save implies that one should not borrow except as a last resort, that one should pay with cash and not on time. But the whole economy of the United States is based upon a credit rather than cash nexus, and only instalment purchasing permits today's production lines to work at their top speed.

Yesterday's worker prided himself upon being a craftsman and with turning out a product that was solid and durable; today obsolescence must be built into the product. Otherwise, its very quality can act as a brake upon the replenishing process to which the production lines are geared, and thereby throw men out of work. In such a situation, to which should people assign a higher moral standard: quality or quantity? Were the older values wrong? To what extent have they become irrelevant? Whatever the answer, the technological order already has created the need for a fundamental reëxamination of traditional attitudes in order to test their continuing validity.

Education—for What?

We have alluded elsewhere to the acceleration of knowledge that is taking place in today's world. Consequently, in economically advanced countries, the traditional educational problem of a scarcity of knowledge and means for its dissemination has been replaced by a more sophisticated challenge: a plethora of both information and misinformation. This new situation raises unprecedented requirements. On the student's part it requires judging between valid and spurious data; on the educator's part it means differentiating between degrees of relevance in the choice of knowledge to be imparted. Given the concept of *change* as the only permanent factor of the society in which educational systems in the technologically advanced West must function, what should be the appropriate curriculum to meet the changing, and accelerating needs of both society and the individual? In the light of what has already been said, emphasis must be placed upon the increasing role of science and technology, and their impact not only upon the material world but also upon man's intellectual outlook, his analytical methods, and his societal values. At the same time, a properly balanced curriculum must ensure that any greater emphasis upon science and its methods is not achieved at the expense of those disciplines which safeguard and enhance the dignity and uniqueness of the individual and the preservation of humanistic values.

Here a further problem arises. Given the indisputable evidence that the acceleration of knowledge quickens the tendency for data to become obsolete, is there not something innately self-defeating in emphasizing the teaching of strictly factual information, especially as an end in itself? Certainly any given discipline has its own corpus of basic factual data, methodological tools, and analytical objectives, and these must be rigorously imparted to all who would master that discipline. But people also need to acquire a new conceptual approach to the educational process itself. The process must not stop with the accumulation of data known at the time it is imparted to the student; beyond this, it must stimulate on his part what has been termed "purposeful self-direction." In other words, he can be taught to recognize problems and relationships arising out of the corpus of factual information, a learning process which activates meaningful responses so as to seek solutions. It is fashionable in some quarters to regard the computer with mixed awe and fear, but only the educated individual can acquire the self-direction capable of recognizing and solving problems that are purposeful within an ever-changing society. In this way, we can answer unequivocally a crucial question posed earlier. Man should, and can, remain autonomous. Indeed, to the extent that an individual permits himself to be made an automaton, he is neither educated nor a man.

That educational systems in economically advanced societies must emphasize purposeful self-direction is also borne out by the challenge of leisure resulting from automation and the reduction of the average work week. At one time, the prospect of obtaining any real freedom from work was limited to a small minority. Americans living at the end of the century, however, will experience hundreds of billions of leisure hours more than they enjoyed in 1950. In fact, not only will the work week be drastically reduced but automation may also eliminate repetitive jobs so rapidly that the government could actually have to pay citizens a guaranteed annual wage for *not* working. What will they do with this leisure? Many look forward expectantly to eternity, but are lost as to what to do on a rainy Sunday afternoon. Of course, Americans might spend all their leisure time at the stadium or before the television set; however, an endless fare of professional sports and situation-comedies-interlarded-with-commercials will eventually reduce most to unrelieved boredom. What is the American educational system doing to prepare its citizens for what we might call "purposeful self-direction" in this expanding area of leisure, since it is precisely here that society must witness a massive confrontation between the technological and humanistic orders?

Let us not become overly pessimistic about man's capacity to cope with these new challenges. The shallowness of the average television program and the obvious phoniness of the accompanying cigarette commercial reflect the inherently contemptuous attitude of the "depth men" whose probing into consumer attitudes (and gullibility) is designed to exploit society's lowest common denominators in order to sell soup or soap. Fortunately, the vast majority of people are neither the fools nor the boors which some take them to be. It is salutary to note that the current population explosion is being matched in the United States and elsewhere by what has been accurately described as a "cultural explosion". Never before have so many Americans enrolled in college, attended concerts, bought serious books and classical records; never before have they patronized on such a scale the public libraries, the art galleries, and the centers for the performing arts which are mushrooming in North American cities. Until this century, art was the private preserve of the aristocracy and the wealthy who alone could afford to play the role of patrons. Today, the patronage and appreciation alike of the arts have acquired an increasingly broad social base. Moreover, people are testing the proposition that the highest quality of artistic expression—and of individual creativity among citizens in school and in community centers—can be compatible with the values and interests of a mass society.

Americans have a long way to go before they resolve the conflicting motives and objectives of the individual's birthright of freedom and the masses' claims for organization, but they can take heart.

This country [the United States] is being watched by peoples—many of them as new to nationhood as they are old in cultural achievements—who ask whether under such a system as ours the highest values can be maintained. It is being watched—and judged. Among our own people, meanwhile, there is a deep and persistent questioning about the significance of our material advance. The ultimate dedication to our way of life will be won not on the basis of economic satisfactions alone, but on the basis of an inward quality and an ideal. Among much that on the surface appears to be complacency or materialism, the Americans —the younger generation especially—are looking for something at once more demanding and more genuinely satisfying than what passes for happiness by current standards. To minimize or frustrate this quest is to risk weakening the fabric of our whole society.[3]

Topics for Discussion:

1. Do you accept the criticism of this age as one dominated by the "commonplace mind"? Examine both sides of the issue.
2. Discuss the differences between technology as a body of material objects and processes, and the "technological order."
3. Is "gigantism" an inevitable corollary of our political, economic, and social activities in today's world? Explain.
4. Do you believe that contemporary man is basically autonomous or an automaton? How do you classify yourself? Defend your position.
5. Does American society gain or lose more from mass acceptance of the dominant role and power of commercial advertising? What do you think life in the U.S.A. would be like without commercial advertising?
6. Discuss Ralph Waldo Emerson's dictum, "Whoso would be a man must be a nonconformist." Is Emerson or today's "well-adjusted" undergraduate closer to the main stream of American social philosophy?
7. Consider the high incidence of alcoholism, suicide, and crimes of violence in contemporary Western societies. Do you ascribe these figures to more comprehensive statistics-gathering, or to a fundamental breakdown in social values and traditional behavior patterns?
8. Discuss science's challenge to traditional religious beliefs. Is religion superfluous or, instead, is it indispensable to the salvation of man from gadgetry and a materialism which seems to regard the universe as pointless, if not absurd?
9. To what extent are the values of thrift, sobriety, and hard work— summed up in the phrase "Puritan ethic"—still appropriate in the technologically-oriented, mass-consumer society of the United States?

Epilogue

In the 1960's, newspaper headlines luridly proclaim numerous antagonisms between national groups, escalating brush-fire wars, confrontations between rival ideologies, and the bewilderments of often-manipulated individuals in societies whose nature and forces they seemed unable to understand or control. But problems are not a new feature of human history. Every step of man, as he has ventured forward, has been attended by dangers and problems. History shows that this journey has never halted for long; man has sidestepped, hurdled, or removed the obstacles in his path. It may be asserted with much justification that these obstructions have been the essential irritants forcing purposeful rumination and action without which mankind would have become complacent and perhaps even decadent.

We know that "without vision the people perish." And there can be little vision without the human strivings and aspirations which are the essential concomitants of problem-solving. What is new in our contemporary world is not the existence of problems but mankind's more acute awareness of them. There is an appreciation, furthermore, of their incongruity in the present stage of civilization. But as problems are eliminated others will take their place. Thus the never-ending challenge to mankind will continue. In ruminating on this historic and inevitable process one of the great philosophers, Alfred North Whitehead (1861-1947), has written:

One main factor in the upward trend of animal life has been the power of wandering . . . Animals wander into new conditions. They have to adapt themselves or die. Mankind has wandered from the trees to the plains, from the plains to the seacoast, from climate to climate, from continent to continent, and from habit of life to habit of life. When man ceases to wander, he will cease to ascend in the scale of being. Physical wandering is still important, but greater still is the power of man's spiritual adventures. . . .

The very benefit of wandering is that it is dangerous . . . the future will disclose dangers . . . pessimism over the future of the world comes from a confusion between civilisation and security. In the immediate future there will be less security than in the immediate past, less stability. . . . But, on the whole, the great ages have been the unstable ages.[1]

FOOTNOTES

INTRODUCTION

1. Albert Camus, *L'Etranger* (New York: Pantheon, 1963), p. 45.
2. See, for example, T. W. Wallbank, A. M. Taylor, G. B. Carson, Jr., *Civilization Past and Present* "Epilogue," vol. 2, fifth edition (Chicago: Scott, Foresman, 1965).

2 NATIONALISM AND EXPANDING LOYALTIES

1. Elizabeth Wallace, "The West Indies Federation: Decline and Fall," *International Journal*, Toronto: vol. 17, no. 3 (Summer, 1962), p. 284.

3 THE POLITICS OF NEW NATIONS: THE EROSION OF WESTERN DEMOCRACY

1. Michael Brecher, *The New States of Asia* (New York: Oxford University Press, 1963), p. 54.

4 SOCIETAL WRONGS AND HUMAN RIGHTS

1. Cited in Gill Evans, "Partition and South Africa's Future." *International Affairs*, New York: vol. 18, no. 2, 1962, p. 246.

6 NATURAL RESOURCES: FUTURE PLENTY OR PENURY?

1. Harrison Brown, quoted in United Nations, *World of Opportunity, Science and Technology for Development*, vol. 1 (New York: United Nations, 1963), p. 19.
2. Rachel Carson, *The Silent Spring* (Boston: Houghton Mifflin, 1962), p. 15.

7 TECHNOLOGY'S POSSIBILITIES AND PROBLEMS

1. F. C. Mann, "Psychological and Organizational Impacts," *Automation and Technological Change*, p. 65.

8 THE INDIVIDUAL IN MASS SOCIETY

1. Ortega y Gasset, *The Revolt of the Masses* (London: Unwin Books, George Allen and Unwin, 1961), p. 14.
2. Herbert J. Muller, *The Individual in a Revolutionary World* (Toronto: Ryerson Press, 1964), p. 32.
3. August Heckscher, "The Quality of American Culture," *Goals for Americans* (Englewood Cliffs: Prentice-Hall, 1964), pp. 145-146.

EPILOGUE

1. Albert North Whitehead, *Science and the Modern World* (New York: New American Library, 1953), pp. 207-208.

SUGGESTIONS FOR FURTHER READING

An asterisk indicates a book is a paperback.

1

Brzezinski, Z. K., *The Soviet Bloc: Unity and Conflict*, re. ed. Praeger, 1961.*

Camps, Miriam, *Britain and the European Community, 1955-1963*. Princeton Univ. Press, 1964.

Floyd, D., *Mao Against Khrushchev*. Praeger, 1964.

Foster, Kent, *Recent Europe*. Ronald Press, 1965.

Griffith, William E., *The Sino-Soviet Rift*. M.I.T. Press, 1964.*

Kissinger, Henry A., *The Necessity for Choice; Prospects of Amer. Foreign Policy*. Harper, 1961.

Rothschild, Joseph, *Communist Eastern Europe*. Walker, 1964.

Steel, Ronald, *The End of Alliance: America and the Future of Europe*. Viking, 1964.

Stillman, E. O., *Bitter Harvest: The Intellectual Revolt Against the Iron Curtain*. Praeger, 1959.

Willis, F. Roy, *France, Germany, and the New Europe*. Stanford University Press, 1964.

2

Crimeans, C., *The Arabs and the World: Nasser's Arab Nationalist Policy*. Praeger, 1963.

Freymond, Jacques, *Western Europe Since the War*. Praeger, 1964.

Laqueur, Walter, ed., *The Middle East in Transition*. Praeger, 1958.

Legume, Colin, *Pan-Africanism*. Praeger, 1962.

Lichtheim, G., *The New Europe*. Praeger, 1963.

Nkrumah, K., *Africa Must Unite*. Praeger, 1963.

Taylor, Alastair M., *Indonesian Independence and the United Nations*. Cornell Univ. Press, 1960.

Wade, Mason, *Canadian Dualism*. University of Toronto Press, 1962.

Wallbank, T. Walter, *1947: Partition in India*. D. C. Heath, 1965.

3

Carter, Gwendolen M., ed., *African One-Party States*. Cornell University Press, 1962.

Crozier, Brian, *The Morning After: A Study of*

Independence. Oxford University Press, 1963.

Fall, Bernard, *The Two Viet-Nams.* Praeger, 1963.

Hanna, Willard A., *Bung Karno's Indonesia.* American Universities Field Staff, 1961.

Harison, Selig A., *India: The Most Dangerous Decades.* Princeton University Press, 1960.

Lamb, Beatrice Pitney, *India: A World in Transition.* Praeger, 1963.

Spiro, J., *Politics in Africa.* Prentice-Hall, 1962.

Wallbank, T. Walter, *Documents on Modern Africa; and Contemporary Africa.* Van Nostrand, 1964.

4

Carter, Gwendolen M., *The Politics of Inequality.* London: Thames and Hudson, 1958.

King, Martin Luther, Jr., *Why We Can't Wait.* New American Library, 1964.*

Lamb, Beatrice Pitney, *India: A World in Transition.* Praeger, 1963.*

Lewis, Anthony, *Portrait of a Decade: The Second American Revolution.* Random House, 1964.

Merton, Robert K., and Nisbet, Robert A., *Contemporary Social Problems.* Harcourt, Brace and World, 1961.

Myrdal, Gunnar, *An American Dilemma: The Negro Problem and Modern Democracy.* Harper and Row, 1963.

Neame, L. E., *The History of Apartheid.* London: Pall Mall Press, 1962.

Simpson, G. E., and Yinger, J. M., *Racial and Cultural Minorities: An Analysis of Prejudices and Discrimination.* Harper and Brothers, 1960.

Wallbank, T. Walter, *Contemporary Africa: Continent in Transition.* Van Nostrand, 1964.*

Zinkin, Taya, *Caste Today.* London: Oxford University Press, 1962.*

5

Chandrasekhar, S., *Hungry People and Empty Lands.* London: George Allen & Unwin, 1954.

Hauser, Philip M., ed., *The Population Dilemma.* Prentice-Hall, 1964.*

Mudd, Stuart, ed., *The Population Crisis and the Use of World Resources.* The Hague: Dr. W. Junk, 1964.

Thompson, Warren S., *Population and Progress in the Far East.* University of Chicago Press, 1959.

United Nations, *Science and Technology for Development,* vol. 5. United Nations, 1963.

6

Boyko, Hugo, ed., *Science and the Future of Mankind.* The Hague: Dr. W. Junk, 1961.

Carson, R., *Silent Spring.* Houghton Mifflin, 1962.

De Castro, Josué, *Geography of Hunger.* Little Brown, 1952.

Landsberg, Hans H., *Natural Resources for U.S. Growth: A Look Ahead to the Year 2000.* The Johns Hopkins Press, 1964.

Mudd, Stuart, ed., *The Population Crisis and the Use of World Resources.* The Hague: Dr. W. Junk, 1964.

Putnam, Palmer C., *Energy in the Future.* Van Nostrand, 1956.

Schurr, Sam H., and Netschert, Bruce C., *Energy in the American Economy 1850-1975: Its History and Prospects.* The Johns Hopkins Press, 1960.

United Nations, *Science and Technology for Development,* vol. 2. United Nations, 1963.

7

Bloomfield, Lincoln P., and others, *International Military Forces: The Question of Peacekeeping in an Armed and Disarming World.* Little Brown, 1964.*

Bloomfield, Lincoln P., ed., *Outer Space: Prospects for Man and Society.* Prentice-Hall, 1962.*

Dunlop, John T., ed., *Automation and Technological Change.* Prentice-Hall, 1962.*

Henkin, Louis, ed., *Arms Control: Issues for the Public.* Prentice-Hall, 1961.*

The President's Commission on National Goals, ed., *Goals for Americans.* Prentice-Hall, 1960.*

Price, Derek J. de Solla, *Science Since Babylon.* Yale University Press, 1961.

United Nations, *Science and Technology for Development,* vol. 7. United Nations, 1963.

Ward, Barbara, *The Rich Nations and the Poor Nations.* W. W. Norton, 1962.*

8

Dupré, J. S., and Lakoff, S. A., *Science and the Nation, Policy and Politics.* Prentice-Hall, 1962.*

Gasset, Ortega y, *The Revolt of the Masses.* London: Unwin Books, 1961.*

Huxley, Aldous, *Brave New World.* Bantam.

Northrop, F. S. C., *Man, Nature and God.* Pocket Books, 1963.*

Polanyi, Michael, *Science, Faith, and Society.* University of Chicago Press, 1964.*

The President's Commission on National Goals, ed., *Goals for Americans.* Prentice-Hall, 1964.*

Thompson, Sir George, *The Foreseeable Future.* Viking Press, 1960.*

United Nations, *Education and Training,* in *Science and Technology for Development,* vol. 6. United Nations, 1963.

Wiener, Norbert, *The Human Use of Human Beings: Cybernetics and Society.* Doubleday, 1954.*